THE SIX VIRTUES OF THE EDUCATED PERSON

Helping Kids to Learn, Schools to Succeed

J. Casey Hurley

ROWMAN & LITTLEFIELD EDUCATION
A division of
ROWMAN & LITTLEFIELD PUBLISHERS, INC.
Lanham • New York • Toronto • Plymouth, UK

Published by Rowman & Littlefield Education
A division of Rowman & Littlefield Publishers, Inc.
A wholly owned subsidiary of The Rowman & Littlefield Publishing Group, Inc.
4501 Forbes Boulevard, Suite 200, Lanham, Maryland 20706
http://www.rowmaneducation.com

Estover Road, Plymouth PL6 7PY, United Kingdom

British Library Cataloguing in Publication Information Available

Library of Congress Cataloging-in-Publication Data

Hurley, J. Casey, 1952–
The six virtues of the educated person : helping kids to learn, schools to succeed / J. Casey Hurley.
    p. cm.
Includes bibliographical references.
ISBN 978-1-60709-274-2 (cloth : alk. paper) — ISBN 978-1-60709-275-9 (pbk. : alk. paper) — ISBN 978-1-60709-276-6 (ebook)
1. Public schools--United States. 2. Education and state—United States. 3. Education—Philosophy. I. Title. LA217.2.H866 2009
    371.010973—dc22
                                2009015580
∞ ™ The paper used in this publication meets the minimum requirements of American National Standard for Information Sciences—Permanence of Paper for Printed Library Materials, ANSI/NISO Z39.48-1992.

Printed in the United States of America

CONTENTS

LIST OF FIGURES

FOREWORD

Casey Hurley advances a straightforward and easily understood premise: *Schools don't change, primarily because they do not have a deep purpose translatable into function, governance, and ultimately structure.* He reminds us that the traditional sequence of steps surrounding creating models for better schools runs something like:

1. Formulate a core belief.
2. Determine governance from the belief.
3. Derive a set of purposes that emanate from the structure.
4. Develop an organizational structure that is connected to purposes.
5. Create an improvement model that is connected to the organizational structure.

After considerable thought, Hurley makes a simple but profound adjustment in these steps. First, he spends more time on core beliefs, fleshing them out to include such things as helping students develop imagination, strong character, courage, humility, and generosity. In this step, Hurley moves beyond the dominant social science model that eliminates such virtues because they are unmeasurable and that is only concerned with easily assessable behaviors. Next, he moves to purposes that include a broader core than normally defined and then connects these to governance. At this juncture, he shifts the focus from political ends to educational ends.

At the next stage, Hurley declines to adopt the usual bureaucratic apparatus into which school reform is normally centered, preferring instead to adopt the notion of a caring, inclusive community, which is a flatter, more democratic notion.

Finally, he creates an improvement paradigm that includes the aesthetic dimensions of human development and not simply the utilitarian benchmarks that have so often led to the "drill and kill" teaching method that has reduced schools to Weber's "iron cage" in which the human spirit has so often been sacrificed.

What is important about this book is not only that Hurley so clearly makes his case for a different reform approach but that, as a thoughtful educator, he gives form and content to the ideas of so many teachers and administrators toiling in schools today who see the destructive effects of mass standardized testing but have not had the luxury of stepping back from the workplace to reconceptualize how it might be different, though their "gut" tells them that there has to be a better way.

We should be indebted to Casey Hurley for thoughtfully indicating a better way. It is my hope that this book receives the kind of consideration that it deserves.

Fenwick W. English
School of Education
The University of North Carolina at Chapel Hill

INTRODUCTION

I was reading student papers on a flight to Montego Bay when the man seated next to me asked if I was a teacher. I explained that I teach school administration in western North Carolina, and I was on my way to do the same in Jamaica.

He said he did professional training too. I sensed that he wanted to talk about shared interests, so I said something like this:

I have a theory about teaching that goes back to my days as a basketball coach. The best coaches keep the fundamental principles in the forefront of their teaching. For example, they realize the laws of geometry and physiology apply to basketball, just as they do to soccer.

Soccer coaches teach their players to pass the ball in a pattern, from the side to the middle, and back to the side so geometry and physiology work in their favor. Players can accept a pass while their bodies are facing the goal, which gives them the best opportunity to create a good angle for attack.

Successful basketball coaches teach this same idea and keep it at the center of their offensive strategies. Mediocre coaches ignore this idea and teach the peripheral strategies they learn in coaching journals, books, and clinics.

The man smiled. He said it was also his experience that the best teachers stick to the essence.

This book is based on the same idea. Successful education sticks to the essence of what it means to be educated.

The following chapters explain two ways of thinking about improving American public education—the way we think about it now, and how we ought to think about it. The first is captured in our current model of schooling. It is a model driven by the politics of education and the findings of educational research—both of which ignore the essential question of what it means to be educated.

The second way is captured in the alternative model presented in chapter 3. This model sticks to the essence by defining the educated person as one who develops understanding and imagination (intellectual virtues), strong character and courage (character virtues), and humility and generosity (spiritual virtues). Comparing the alternative model with our current one explains the educational significance of these virtues.

Chapter 1 explains our current model of public education. Understanding is deepened by seeing the model's focus, the relationships among the five elements of schooling, and the assumptions underlying those relationships.

Chapter 2 provides a history of how three of the elements have driven public education and how we have found ourselves where we are today. We need a deep understanding of history before deciding to either improve or replace our current model.

Chapter 3 describes an alternative model. It starts with the six-virtue definition of the educated person. This is the essence that focuses schooling on educational beliefs and purposes instead of political ones.

Chapters 4 through 8 describe the alternative elements in greater detail. This model departs from our current one in several ways, but the two most significant departures are in the core belief that drives everything and in the relationship between governance and purpose.

Chapter 9 and the epilogue explain how we can move from our current model to the alternative. It will not be easy. Implementing a new model of education requires the modeling and teaching of all six virtues.

Some ideas in this book are familiar to those who study American education. Others are not. The familiar ideas are that public education

(1) is driven by politics, (2) serves a public interest, (3) strives to improve standardized test scores, (4) and is bureaucratically structured.

This book's unique contributions to the school improvement literature are the following:

1. Our educated human nature demonstrates the virtues of understanding, imagination, strong character, courage, humility, and generosity.
2. Our uneducated human nature demonstrates the opposite vices of ignorance, intellectual incompetence, weakness, fear, pride, and selfishness.
3. These vices and virtues can be separated in discussion but not in human behavior or situations.
4. Today's public schools teach three of the virtues (understanding, strong character, and generosity) and three of the vices (intellectual incompetence, fear, and pride).
5. Educated (virtuous) people make life beautiful, and uneducated ones make it ugly.
6. The democratic governance of education is antieducational because it models and promotes the six vices.
7. Virtue purposes are more fundamental, more comprehensive, and more useful than knowledge and skill purposes.
8. The operation of American public education can be captured in a model that includes a core belief, a governance approach, a set of purposes, an organizational structure, and an improvement paradigm. Relationships among these elements are explained in chapter 1.

The alternative model and the six-virtue definition of the educated person can be unifying themes for a classroom or school. They can be founding principles for a parochial, charter, or independent school. Or they can guide what parents teach their children. As this happens, the credit goes to those who embrace this vision of a better world. The benefits accrue to our children.

1

OUR CURRENT MODEL OF PUBLIC SCHOOLING

Models can deepen understanding by showing how a concept's parts relate to each other. A model airplane is a good example. Although the model itself does not fly, the relationships among the different parts suggest that a machine with two wings and a fuselage in specific proportions can be lifted by air traveling beneath the wings. Similarly, a model of an educational system illustrates how its various parts relate to each other.

Models can also frame things in a way that focuses on the essence. An example is a photograph that frames the subject within the foreground or background. Similarly, an educational model can focus educators and students on the essence of what it means to be educated.

Models can expose underlying assumptions. For example, the organizational chart of a bureaucratic hierarchy is a model that exposes the assumption that only supervised employees satisfactorily perform their duties. This assumption is evident wherever the chart holds a place for those whose primary responsibility is to supervise others.

Figure 1.1 illustrates the five elements of our current model of public schooling. The arrows suggest ways in which the elements relate to each other. Its shape frames public education around a core belief. And analyzing the model exposes some of the assumptions underlying both the relationships and the core belief.

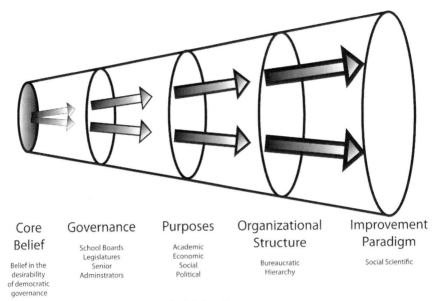

Core Belief	Governance	Purposes	Organizational Structure	Improvement Paradigm
Belief in the desirability of democratic governance	School Boards Legislatures Senior Adminstrators	Academic Economic Social Political	Bureaucratic Hierarchy	Social Scientific

Figure 1.1. **Our Current Model of Schooling** Neil Torda

ELEMENTS OF OUR CURRENT MODEL

The five elements are

- A core belief that drives everything
- A democratic form of governance
- Purposes established by elected officials
- A bureaucratic organizational structure
- A social science improvement paradigm

The first •element is our belief in the desirability of democratic governance. It is represented by the oval farthest to the left. According to Andrew Newberg, "The brain is a believing machine because it has to be. Beliefs affect every part of our lives. They make us who we are. They are the essence of our being" (Loviglio, 2007).

A belief in the desirability of democratic governance drives public education, and the rest of the model flows naturally from it. As Newberg would say, it affects every part of public education.

The second oval represents our democratic approach to governing public education. We govern in a way that emerges from both our core belief and our desire to model democratic governance to young people.

The third oval represents public school purposes established by elected officials. Early in the common school movement, proponents of taxpayer-funded education argued that public schools would serve both public and private purposes. Public purposes would prepare citizens for employment and democratic citizenship. Private ones would provide individuals with educational, social, and career opportunities.

Cuban (1984, p. 247) believes public purposes are "the true purposes of the institution, i.e. social control, and sorting of students into economic niches." Over the past 30 years, these "true purposes" have been increasingly influenced by state and federal politics. The No Child Left Behind (NCLB) legislation signed in 2002 is the culmination of efforts to centralize the governance of public education.

The fourth oval represents the bureaucratic organizational structure of public education. By hiring administrators to evaluate and supervise school personnel, elected officials hold school personnel accountable for the achievement of educational purposes and for the proper use of public funds.

The fifth oval represents our school improvement paradigm. The concept of an improvement paradigm is integral to education models, so further explanation is needed.

"Paradigm" is used in its Kuhnian sense. The *Oxford Dictionary of Social Science* (Calhoun, 2002) defines Kuhn's concept of paradigm:

> the term [paradigm] refers to the general set of assumptions, questions, and methods that structures a field of inquiry at any given time." Together, these define the boundaries of what Kuhn called "normal science." He argued further that paradigms are basically "incommensurable"—each is structured by a distinct logic that guides inquiry, determines the standards of truth, and delimits the range of acceptable answers.

The first sentence explains that paradigms affect what is assumed about a field, what is asked about it, and what is found as it is explored. Our current school improvement paradigm is social scientific because it assumes schools improve when teachers apply the findings of social science research to become more effective. The social science

paradigm is invoked every time an education report states "more research is needed."

Kuhn's concept also explains that different paradigms are "incom-
mensurable." They enable us to see certain things while preventing us
from seeing others. For example, a social science paradigm enables us
to theorize that bee movements communicate pollen locations, but an
aesthetic paradigm is needed to describe those movements as a dance.

RELATIONSHIPS AMONG THE ELEMENTS

The five elements relate to each other in ways that capture the operation of today's public schools. Before describing those relationships,
however, some might ask, "Why these five elements? Couldn't other
constructs be used to describe public education?"

I am not arguing against all other possible ways to illustrate the operation of public education. Instead, I am arguing that these five elements,
and the relationships among them, form an integrated conceptualization
of how public education actually works. The elements are so integrally
related that each one affects everything else about schooling. Changing
one would affect all the others.

For example, the distribution of educational vouchers would not only
change how public education is governed, but it would also change the
other four elements. The core belief would become one that believes in
the desirability of market forces. And this belief would change schools'
purposes, their organizational structure, and the paradigm for improving them. New purposes would be to attract and retain voucher-carry-
ing students. The new organizational chart would include positions for
marketing experts. And improvement would be achieved by enrolling
more capable students.

These elements also coincide with the following American beliefs
about democracy and public education:

- Democratic governance is desirable.
- Public education should be governed democratically.
- Elected officials should establish public school purposes.

- Public school personnel should be organized in a bureaucratic hierarchy.
- Educational research findings should be used to improve schools.

The veracity of these beliefs is challenged in chapters 4 through 9. For now, it is important to see that figure 1.1 is a model that captures these beliefs and illustrates their interrelatedness in our current system of public education.

The arrows start at the core belief and shoot to the right—suggesting that the elements on the left influence those to the right. The most fundamental element is our belief in the desirability of democratic governance. Because of this belief, elected officials establish educational purposes. Further to the right, bureaucratic hierarchy emerges from the need for elected officials to hold school personnel accountable for achieving those purposes. And farthest to the right, the social science paradigm emerges from the belief that senior administrators should use research findings to lead school improvement efforts.

The increasing boldness of the arrows as they pass through the elements suggests another relationship. The influences on the relationships on the right side of the figure are easier to see than those on the left.

It is easy to see that bureaucratic hierarchy requires an improvement paradigm that relies on experts outside the school. Teachers occupy the bottom rung of the education bureaucracy. According to bureaucratic principles, policymakers and senior administrators cannot trust subordinates (teachers) to improve schools, so they look outside the bureaucracy for improvement guidance. Educational researchers are the obvious choice because they are considered experts in the field.

When I was a public high school administrator, I often sat in the audience of school board meetings in which elected officials made school improvement decisions. Those of us who were principals and teachers were largely excluded from discussions, but board members frequently asked the superintendent, "What does the research say?" Evidently they valued the experiences of social scientists who had never been in their local schools more than the experiences of the professionals who worked in them every day.

My colleagues thought this was appropriate because all their education experience had been in public schools. They shared the assumption that policymakers and senior administrators should use the findings of educational research to direct school personnel on how to improve schools. I did not share this assumption because I had experiences in Catholic schools, where teachers were largely responsible for school improvement.

Every time a school board member asks "What does the research say?" it is easy to see that bureaucratic hierarchy promotes the social science improvement paradigm.

It is more difficult to see that politically established purposes promote bureaucratic hierarchy. With a little insight, however, it can be seen that elected officials do not have the time to hold teachers accountable. Therefore, a bureaucratic organizational structure is created and senior administrators are hired to supervise them.

It takes effort to see this because policymakers do not admit they cannot hold teachers accountable and administrators do not admit they are hired to carry out this function. The rhetoric of education administrators constantly refers to "supporting," "facilitating," and "leading," so it is difficult to see that bureaucracy requires them to mistrust teachers and principals, or to hold them accountable.

Further to the left, it is more difficult to see that governance from the state and federal levels has focused public education on purposes that ignore the needs of individual students. For example, today's focus on preparing students for participation in the global economy of the 21st century does not address the more immediate needs of students, such as the need for a learning environment that affords the right amounts of academic, personal, and social challenges. These needs can only be addressed by local educators and policymakers

But this is difficult to see because we believe all forms of democratic governance are desirable. If local democratic governance is desirable, state and federal democracy is even more desirable. This belief is clear in the expectation that federal policies supersede state ones, and state policies supersede local ones.

Finally, the most difficult relationship to see is that our belief in the desirability of democracy causes us to govern democratically. Several years ago one of my graduate students helped me see this.

When I asked the class if public education would be fundamentally different in the year 2030, he said it would not because democratic governance maintains stability and resists reform and revolution. Therefore, he reasoned, a democratically governed system of public education was unlikely to be fundamentally different in 2030.

I thank my graduate student for seeing this, and I wonder why others do not. Many times the same policymakers and education scholars who call for the reform of public education also insist that it be democratically governed. They are unable to see what my graduate student saw—our belief in democratic governance ensures stability and prevents reform.

Another relationship expressed by the two arrows is the differing perspectives of public school personnel and elected officials. The distance between the two arrows represents these differences. As we look at the elements on the left and move to those on the right, the two groups increasingly disagree with each other.

The arrows are anchored at the same point on the left because both groups share the core belief in the desirability of democratic governance. Regarding the practice of governance, however, they begin to move apart.

As mentioned earlier, school boards sometimes govern without consulting those who work in the schools. Principals and teachers accept this because few board policies affect their day-to-day responsibilities.

Disagreements begin to emerge, however, when policymakers try to influence daily operations. For example, teachers and principals resent classroom visits from school board members, and board members resent being kept out of schools and classrooms. In other words, policymakers and school personnel disagree on how to share governance.

When it comes to purpose, disagreements are even greater. This is evident in the NCLB goal that states all students should be at grade level by 2014. Teachers and principals realize this is impossible (Brulle, 2005; Rothstein, Jacobsen, & Wilder, 2006). Even more so, they realize that, for some children, performing at grade level is one of the least important issues in their lives. Clearly, the groups disagree more about purposes than they do about governance.

The distance between arrows is even greater regarding organizational structure. Bureaucratic hierarchy gives control of resources to policymakers and administrators farthest away from students. This creates situations in which teachers and elected officials disagree more strongly.

One day, when I was volunteering in a public school classroom, my host teacher expressed such a disagreement. She had just completed a postobservation conference, and she felt insulted by the supervisory experience. Just before I was about to leave, she approached me and asked, rhetorically, "How can they assess my teaching when they come in only three times a year? Isn't this a huge waste of resources? They pay these people's salaries but they take away our teaching assistants."

Scarce resources are spent this way because the public school bureaucracy assumes teachers cannot be trusted to satisfactorily perform their duties. But teachers regard themselves as trustworthy professionals, so they disagree with spending resources this way.

Finally, disagreements between the two groups are greatest concerning the school improvement paradigm. Earlier I mentioned that school board members base policy decisions on the findings of educational research. They assume what Cochran-Smith (2002, p. 284) called the "research as foundation" metaphor:

> It is assumed first that there is a body of knowledge based on cutting-edge empirical research in various academic disciplines that is relevant to teaching, learning, and schooling, and second, that when teachers know and act on this knowledge, schooling is more effective.

Teachers and principals, however, rarely look to research to improve their practice because they know educational research is deeply rooted in politics. Allington (2005, p. 464) described a recent "reading wars" example:

> There was a substantial mismatch between what the NRP [National Reading Panel] actually found and what the Summary of the NRP report said the panel found. . . . The errors in the reporting of findings reflect, to my mind, a simple ideological bias in favor of a particular sort of reading instruction for beginning readers and for struggling readers—the sort of reading instruction that the full report doggedly avoided recommending.

The arrows are farthest apart as they pass through the school improvement paradigm because elected officials expect school personnel to apply research findings to improve their schools, but teachers and principals pay little attention to research. Instead, they improve schools by using judgment to deal with specific students in specific situations.

In summary, figure 1.1 portrays several relationships among the elements. First, the order of the elements is such that those to the left influence those to the right. Second, the increasing boldness of the arrows suggests that it is easier to see that a social scientific improvement paradigm emerges from bureaucratic hierarchy than it is to see that democratic governance emerges from a core belief. Third, the increasing gap between the arrows illustrates that disagreements between policymakers and school personnel are greater in the elements farthest to the right.

FRAMING PUBLIC EDUCATION

This model focuses the eye on the core belief. We Americans believe in the desirability of democratic governance, but beyond that, we agree little about how to operate public schools. Some reformers call for changing how we govern (vouchers and other choice initiatives). Others call for new purposes (get back to basics or prepare students to compete in the global economy of the 21st century). Others suggest new organizational structures (site-based decision making or learning communities). And all of their ideas are driven by research that is political and unscientific (McClintock, 2007).

The point is that figure 1.1 does not focus our thinking about public education or our efforts to improve it. It suggests that our thinking about education is scattered, like the buckshot from a shotgun.

ASSUMPTIONS ABOUT PUBLIC SCHOOLING

Stephanie Pace Marshall referred to our assumptions about public education in her 1998 presidential address to the Association for Supervision and Curriculum Development (ASCD) national conference:

It is clear that a large part of the story that we had so logically written about human systems and human organizations—and places called schools—are grounded in false and disabling assumptions about human beings and our learning, and they are casting a malignant shadow over the human spirit. (cited in Brown & Moffett, 1999, p. 156)

Our core belief in the desirability of democratic governance is one of the most "false and disabling" of these assumptions. It turns out that political governance, even that which is democratic, is antieducational.

In *The Prince*, Machiavelli described politics as the ruthless use of power. According to Sahakian (1968, p. 121), Machiavelli believed that

> In politics, *the end justifies the means*, any means, no matter how deceitful, lawless, or unscrupulous. If a person successfully achieves highest political power, then it is of little consequence how he achieved it because the masses who allow themselves to be deceived, will then obey and respect their ruler.

To what extent is public education governed in accordance with this belief? If the use of ruthless power is promoted in politics, should this be modeled in the education of our young people?

Sahakian (1968, p. 122) described another of Machiavelli's political beliefs this way:

> The political philosophy set forth in *The Prince* is not applicable to a State where citizens are good, but only where they are corrupt. For a society of virtuous persons, he recommends a quite different system, a republic instead of the tyranny espoused in *The Prince*.

Are Americans virtuous enough to sustain a republican form of government? Does our system of public education promote a virtuous citizenry?

When it comes to governing public education, instead of assuming democratic governance is both desirable and necessary, we should consider the possibility that neither is true. It may be that the antieducational nature of American democratic politics disqualifies it as an appropriate way to govern education. It may be that, in order to bring integrity to public education, it must be governed educationally.

Before describing what that looks like in chapters 3 through 8, chapter 2 describes how three elements of our current model have driven public education to where it is today.

2

HOW DID WE GET HERE?

Historians trace the modern period of public education back to the publication of *A Nation at Risk* in 1983. Their descriptions of key events over the past 25 years enhance our understanding of how public education has been driven toward our current situation. I will not duplicate their descriptions here. Instead, this chapter describes how governance has been centralized, how bureaucracy prevents reform of public education, and how we should question the epistemological assumptions of the social science improvement paradigm.

The first section discusses how centralized governance has affected public school purposes and why this shift met with so little resistance. The second section describes how professional norms and the rules of bureaucratic hierarchy extend the education bureaucracy to the federal level. The third section explains how the social science improvement paradigm benefits those who work outside the schools more than those who work inside them.

FROM LOCAL TO CENTRAL GOVERNANCE

Today's federally established purposes focus schools on training a global workforce, which means having students' standardized test scores as high or higher than those of students in other countries. After this purpose is addressed, local educators can address the needs of individual students.

Governing from state and federal levels means those responsible for improving public education (teachers, principals, parents, and students) are excluded from policy debates—which is why our purposes have become unbalanced. As teachers pursue higher test scores, they eliminate activities that address students' individual needs. At a time when young people are in need of healthy minds, bodies, and spirits, why have teachers and principals not been able to argue that achieving higher test scores is among the least important of our purposes? One reason is that the educational debate has been moved to the state and federal levels.

Cuban (2003) regards local governance as critical to public education:

> Local autonomy is critical in making choices about what goals to pursue, how to organize schools, and what and how to teach, particularly so in the absence of scientific evidence that one form of schooling is superior to another. Localities differ dramatically and local decision-making offers ways for school boards to tailor their schools to fit particular contexts. (p. 48)

Local governance is needed to keep purposes in balance.

Since the common school movement of the mid-19th century, elected school boards and state legislatures have governed public education. The federal government became involved only when localities and states failed to provide equal educational opportunities. The first time was the 1954 *Brown v. Topeka Board of Education* Supreme Court decision, which ruled that segregated schools were inherently unequal.

Since then, Title IX legislation has required that programming for females be equal to that for males. And Public Law 94-142 has established the principle of providing the least restrictive environment for students with disabilities. Additionally, Congress passed the 1958 National Defense Education Act (NDEA), and the 1965 Elementary and Secondary Education Act (ESEA). The first was a response to Sputnik. The second provided federal funds for the nutritional and academic needs of low-income students.

The 2002 reauthorization of the ESEA, which is known as No Child Left Behind (NCLB), greatly expanded the federal role. Congress and the Bush administration legislated that, in order for states to receive federal funds, public schools must administer tests that determine whether students in different subgroups are making adequate yearly progress, must have highly qualified teachers in every classroom, and must adopt research-based instructional programs.

Even though state systems of education are rooted in different traditions and laws, NCLB requires these three things from all of them. If this law had taken state differences into account, it would have been unwieldy. It also would have been unnecessary because during the 1990s many states had already passed school improvement legislation aimed at improving student test scores.

To be regarded as feasible and necessary, NCLB was based on the premise that all states were in need of all its provisions. The only thing left to negotiate was how each state would determine whether student subgroups were making adequate yearly progress.

Critics of the law describe ways in which it is more harmful than helpful (National Council of Churches Committee on Public Education and Literacy, 2007; Rothstein, Jacobsen, & Wilder, 2006). Why did such a bad idea meet with so little resistance?

The groundwork for this shift was laid by *A Nation at Risk*. I was an assistant principal in 1983, when a colleague came to my office one April morning and said, "The education report in this morning's newspaper is going to change everything." I thought he was exaggerating because he saw political motivations everywhere. But this time he was right. The impact of *A Nation at Risk* is continuing to be felt in America's public schools; and yes—it has changed everything.

Bracey (2003) described the politics surrounding its release. Several members of President Reagan's cabinet criticized it for failing to mention the administration's agenda—"vouchers, tuition tax credits, restoring school prayer, and abolishing the U.S. Department of Education" (Bracey, 2003, p. 617).

But others liked the language that painted the public schools as a failing institution. The most famous sentence of the report read: "If an unfriendly foreign power had attempted to impose on America the mediocre educational performance that exists today, we might well have viewed it as an act of war" (Bracey, 2003, p. 617).

In the most insightful paragraph of the article, Bracey (2003, p. 621) explained that a belief in the failure of public education benefits many interest groups:

> Conservatives want vouchers and tuition tax credits; liberals want more resources for schools; free marketers want to privatize the schools and make money; fundamentalists want to teach religion and not worry about the First Amendment; Catholic schools want to stanch their student hemorrhage; home schooling advocates want just that; and various groups no doubt just want to be with "their own kind." All groups believe that they will improve their chances of getting what they want if they pummel the publics.

One of the reasons NCLB met with so little resistance is that pummeling the "publics" serves the interests of all these groups.

Even if Bracey (2003) exaggerated political motivations, which I don't think he did, one of the great ironies of modern Republican Party politics is that NCLB dramatically increased federal control of public education. How did we go from federal interventions that addressed unequal educational opportunities to those that have specific testing, staffing, and instructional requirements?

The door to federal involvement was opened in 1965 with passage of the ESEA. The door was opened more in 1978 when President Carter established the Department of Education.

Two years later, Reagan won the presidency on a platform that called for abolishing the Department of Education. Throughout the 1980 presidential campaign, Republicans argued that education was a state responsibility.

Although the Department of Education survived the Reagan presidency, public school critics like William Bennett, Tommy Thompson, and corporate CEOs trumpeted the failure of public schools during the 1980s and 1990s. Because of the Republican Party's history of criticizing public schools and of scorning the Department of Education, some believe their sponsorship of NCLB may have been motivated more by a desire to undermine public education than to improve it. Considering the intrusiveness of the law, cynics may have reason to see it that way.

But I am not that cynical. Other reasons NCLB was passed with so little objection pertain to American beliefs about governance and education.

Americans believe democracy is the best way to govern. No matter the values, culture, and traditions of a people, we believe they should govern themselves democratically.

During the 1990s, we also believed we were "a nation at risk" because public schools were not accomplishing their purposes. *A Nation at Risk* spurred local efforts to improve schools. When local officials were unsuccessful in improving student test scores, state legislatures passed school reform laws. When schools still did not improve, Congress passed NCLB. And each step along the way, our belief in the desirability of democratic governance gave hope.

We hoped the right piece of legislation would improve public schools. That is why NCLB met so little resistance. When it comes to school improvement, we believe in simple solutions, and legislation provides them. To legislate school improvement from the federal level, all that was needed was an appealing title and a simple intent. NCLB has both. Who can argue with leaving no child behind? And it certainly would be good if all students were at grade level, if highly qualified teachers were in every classroom, and if teachers effectively used research-based practices.

But the cost of centralized governance is that local educators and policymakers have no voice. The result is a federal intrusion that, at best, creates an imbalance of purposes—and, at worst, destroys the spirits of low-achieving students. The following section describes why this dramatic shift happened with hardly a whimper from the local and state officials who are elected and appointed to govern education.

GOOD INTENTIONS AND RULE #1 OF BUREAUCRATIC HIERARCHY

Bureaucratic hierarchies are based on the assumption that, without supervision, workers cannot be trusted to satisfactorily perform their duties. In the education bureaucracy, the policymakers and senior administrators who supervise teachers and principals are uncomfortable in this role for three reasons. First, they regard teachers and principals as professionals, or at least semiprofessionals. Second, they know teaching and learning are difficult to assess. Third, experience has taught them that most teachers and principals are dedicated to helping children grow and learn.

Many of them react to being uncomfortable by having good intentions as they carry out their mistrusting, supervisory functions. Having good intentions and respecting the good intentions of others is a powerful norm among educational supervisors.

Tyack and Hansot (1982) described the norm this way:

> Although public education has in fact always been an arena where different groups have contended for benefits, it has never developed a consistent ideology to justify such conflict. Both lay and professional leaders have sought common ground and accommodation and regarded conflict as abnormal and undesirable. . . .
>
> With few exceptions, public educators have believed in the soundness of the American social order and the belief systems supporting it, including the value of controlled competition in such domains as politics, religion, and the economy. Within public education, however, they have sought to prevent organized opposition by stressing consensus, by claiming schools should be "above politics," or by absorbing, co-opting, or deflecting outside forces. (p. 10)

Through the expression of one's own good intentions, and by recognizing the good intentions of others, conflict is avoided throughout the public school bureaucracy.

If we combine these good intentions with the realization that schooling for poor children is continuing to fall behind that of middle- and upper-class children (Anyon, 2005; Berliner, 2005), we must ask why good intentions have not produced more benefit for those most in need of public education. To understand the impotence of what should be a powerful force (the good intentions of educational leaders), we need to understand good intentions within the context of a bureaucratic hierarchy.

Bureaucracies have organizational charts in the shape of a triangle. A chief executive is at the top, with vice presidents below, holding subordinates accountable for various aspects of the operation. We are familiar with these organizations because they are prominent in business, politics, education, and religion. What we often ignore about this organizational structure, though, is that its purpose is to make the organization stable.

Stability is often a good thing. I learned the importance of organizational stability during one of my teaching assignments in Jamaica. I was about to mail a note to a Jamaican friend when my students stopped me. They told me mail delivery is so unreliable that few Jamaicans use it.

I compared this idea with my knowledge of the U.S. Postal Service (USPS)—a rigid bureaucracy that provides reliable mail service. The bureaucratic structure of the USPS makes accurate mail delivery a daily event. Americans use it with confidence, and nobody calls for its reform.

But policymakers and education scholars continually call for the reform of public education. And they become frustrated when it resists reform after reform.

They are frustrated because they don't understand the power of bureaucratic hierarchy's Rule #1: "Above all else, preserve the hierarchy." The same rule that provides reliable mail service makes public education impervious to change and improvement.

Former president Bill Clinton learned about Rule #1 from Professor Quigley at Georgetown (Clinton, 2005, pp. 101–102): "The problem, according to Quigley, is that all instruments eventually become 'institutionalized'—that is, vested interests more committed to preserving their own prerogatives than to meeting the needs for which they were created." Boyd (1989) calls this same phenomenon "goal displacement."

Quigley's and Boyd's insights explain that, whenever the self-preserving nature of bureaucracy is stronger than its capacity to achieve organizational goals, the result is a stable organization that fails to achieve the purposes for which it was established. Rule #1 ensures that this happens in bureaucratic organizations.

Public education's bureaucratic organizational structure is dysfunctional because policymakers and senior administrators honor each other's good intentions, follow Rule #1, and blame teachers when schools fail to improve. Cuban (2003, p. 1) put it this way: "Both administrators and policymakers, seeking improvement in student performance, view teachers, paradoxically, as both the problem and the solution to school defects."

Two North Carolina situations illustrate how Rule #1 works, and how it combines with good intentions to maintain a stable, dysfunctional bureaucracy. The first is a news article reporting that the Education Trust found North Carolina "needlessly inflated its high school graduation rate in a report to the federal government" (Morrison, 2003):

> State Superintendent Mike Ward bristled at the notion that North Carolina was purposely painting a rosy scenario. The state complied with federal guidelines while developing a new system for accurately calculating graduation rates, he said.
>
> "For the Education Trust to come along and suggest we're somehow deceitful, it is absolute nonsense," Ward said.
>
> The state reported that 92 percent of its public school students graduated in 2002, while an analysis by the Education Trust concluded the correct figure was closer to 63 percent.

North Carolina reported misleading data, even though both state and federal officials knew they were misleading. When this was pointed out, the state superintendent's reaction was to remind the public of his agency's good intentions. One does not have to be a cynic to see that good intentions and Rule #1 prevented anybody in the bureaucracy from admitting the data were misleading.

The second example occurred during a North Carolina State Department of Public Instruction official's visit to Western Carolina University. When asked why the state was accommodating new federal requirements by undoing policies that were successfully improving test scores, he did not deny the assertion; he said the state could not afford to lose federal funds during a tight budget year.

In other words, North Carolina abandoned what had been successful to accommodate the federal bureaucracy. It received federal funds to operate less beneficial programs than the ones that had been in place. Other states made similar decisions (Mathews & Helderman, 2004).

Is state acquiescence to NCLB improving education? It would take an extensive cost-benefit analysis to answer that question, but it requires no such analysis to recognize that every decision to accommodate NCLB follows Rule #1 and extends bureaucracy to the federal level. Without the courage to stand against the intrusion of NCLB, state officials are left to express their frustration.

According to Morrison (2003), "Ward said North Carolina was working hard to help at-risk students get the help they need for graduation long before No Child Left Behind came along." The state superintendent's point was that state government knows the needs of North Carolina's schools better than the federal government. But he cannot make that argument because, if he argued that the state knows better than the federal, it would follow that the local knows better than the state. Neither argument is made because Rule #1 states "Above all else, preserve the hierarchy."

State officials now feel the mistrust of federal rules, just as local educators have always felt the mistrusting hand of the state. And, because of Rule #1, well-intentioned bureaucrats and state administrators can't do anything about it.

When many are calling for the improvement of public education, are good intentions enough? Good intentions are the makeup on the face of educational politics. Teachers and students are not oppressed by the bad intentions of educational policymakers; they are oppressed by their good intentions.

Adding a layer of federal bureaucracy extends the bureaucratic hierarchy, but it does nothing to improve education for those students most in need of it. Only the efforts of those at the bottom of the organizational chart—teachers, principals, and parents—can address the needs of individual students. They have been silenced, though, by a government and a bureaucracy that now drives public education from the federal level.

THE ROLE OF THE SOCIAL SCIENCE
IMPROVEMENT PARADIGM

One of the elements of our current schooling model is the social science improvement paradigm. When teachers and principals admit that politics drives public education, they are also expressing the belief that education should be driven by social scientific research.

This belief, which is shared by policymakers and educational researchers, is based on the assumption that education is an applied social science. Like researchers in the natural sciences, social science researchers are supposed to fill in knowledge gaps, as if they are putting together a giant picture puzzle. When enough pieces are in place, the final picture will show teachers and principals how to improve schools.

Although this is *not* how schools improve, this paradigm is firmly entrenched in American public education. Its place is made secure by how it serves the interests of policymakers and researchers.

First, it provides a cover of scientific neutrality for politically motivated policymakers. Education research reports never describe the ways in which they are designed to promote certain political points of view, even though they are often designed to do just that (Bracey, 2008; Kohn, 2006). An example is how the Department of Education used education research findings to fund only phonics-based reading programs (Manzo, 2007).

Research is a powerful weapon in the arsenal of education politics. For example, in the "Great Debate" about reading instruction, conservative politicians cite research that finds benefits in phonics-based instruction, while liberal politicians cite research that finds benefits in whole language. The irony is that research designed to support political positions is cited by policymakers as evidence that their positions are "above politics" (Tyack & Hansot, 1982).

This paradigm also serves the interests of those who produce the social science findings. Federal grants and published findings are the path to tenure at most universities.

Some educational researchers admit that their findings are not used by teachers and principals. According to Davis (2007, pp. 569–570):

> It appears that comparatively little of what is written and thought about by scholars and policymakers actually has any appreciable impact on classrooms or drives durable system wide reform efforts. . . .
>
> Of course, not all reform efforts have been research-based, and not all good research is lost in the trickledown journey between the halls of academe and Ms. Doe's third-grade classroom. But enough of value is lost to raise suspicions about the relevance of the work of researchers and the vitality of the relationship between researchers and public school practitioners.

If researchers know their findings rarely inform school practice, how do they respond? Many of them write about the "research–practice divide."

When scholars described this gap in special sections of *Phi Delta Kappan* (April 2007) and *Educational Leadership* (March 2006), they called for practitioners to develop more knowledge about using research, and for researchers to generate more applicable findings. Instead of questioning the assumption upon which their paradigm is based, they called for more of what is ignored in schools.

The epistemological assumptions of this paradigm are not immune from challenge. Social scientists and philosophers like MacIntyre (1981), Greenfield (1986), and Dewey (1938) have argued that the social science of education is a dead end. And Davis (2007) calls for educators to be suspicious of research.

My own suspicions were raised shortly after becoming a high school administrator. I had just completed a master's degree in educational administration from the University of Wisconsin–Madison, where my professors were esteemed social scientists and researchers. In my assistant principal role, however, I rarely referenced their teachings. Instead, I constantly referenced the teachings of my mother—that we should treat others the way we want to be treated, that children learn from the example of adults, and that we all have different gifts.

My mother's teachings were more relevant than my professors'. Ironically, they were also more easily tested in my experience.

This surprised me because, as a graduate student, I believed public education would improve as more pieces of the puzzle were put together. Policymakers and researchers believe this today, which is why NCLB has the "research-based" programming provision.

My suspicions about the relevance of research were deepened in my career as a university professor. One summer I returned to my alma mater to attend a workshop sponsored by the Consortium for Policy Research in Education (CPRE).

As the workshop progressed, I began to feel uncomfortable because one of its purposes was to disseminate findings from a three-year study of how the Charlotte-Mecklenburg School District improved its standardized test scores. CPRE researchers had collected data in North Carolina, and they were suggesting that their findings could inform the practice of workshop attendees, most of whom were Wisconsin public school administrators.

I was uncomfortable because I had lived in both states, and I had intimate knowledge of their different educational systems and the cultures within which these systems are imbedded. North Carolina is a highly centralized system of public education, but Wisconsin has more than 400 autonomous school districts.

During my first five years in North Carolina (1989–1994), the state legislature mandated new programs, provided new funds for specially legislated programs, and even charted new directions for public education. I discovered that North Carolina teachers and principals took state control of education for granted. When I asked them how they felt about state intrusions into their work, they said things like, "We don't pay much attention to state mandates. They change every two years, so we just wait them out."

And this is exactly what happened until 1994, when Republicans gained control of the legislature. Once in control, the new majority threatened to sponsor voucher legislation if Democrats did not join them in holding teachers and principals accountable for improved student test scores. The result was the establishment of a statewide accountability system called the "ABCs of Public Education."

Although North Carolina is highly centralized, it sponsors great funding disparities across school districts. Local property taxes pay for "brick-and-mortar" projects, so high-wealth districts have fine facilities and programs, and low-wealth districts have outdated facilities and little opportunity to make them better.

In comparison, Wisconsin has a tradition of locally controlled public schools. More than 400 school boards govern local programs, curriculum, testing, and facilities. Wisconsin equalizes funding, so property-poor districts are funded at levels close to the state average.

While sitting at the workshop, I wondered if I should comment on the differences between the two states. If I did, what would I say? I decided not to say anything, which was the right thing to do. Nobody wanted to discuss the difficulty of drawing meaningful comparisons between situations in two completely different states.

Instead, researchers wanted to share their findings, and administrators wanted to sit passively, knowing that those findings were irrelevant to their work. I knew they felt that way because, when I was one of them, I also attended workshops and conferences about research findings that were irrelevant to my work.

Teachers and principals don't experience a research–practice divide. Instead, they are confronted with actual situations whose complexities defy the relevance of research findings. For those who work in schools, the truest guide for action is, "In all situations, it depends on the situation." (This idea is explained more in chapter 8.)

When teachers and principals focus on the actual instead of the theoretical, it is not because they are intellectually incompetent, as implied by research scholars who believe there is some type of "research–practice divide." It is because they work in the real world, not the theoretical world. Their work is essentially about the arts of teaching and schooling, but educational research addresses theoretical possibilities at the periphery of their daily work.

CONCLUSION

Three elements of our schooling model have driven us to where we are today:

- Governance is centralized to the point where public education pursues public purposes at the expense of private ones.
- The educational bureaucracy has been extended to the federal level by policymakers and senior administrators who have to follow bureaucratic hierarchy's Rule #1.
- And the social science improvement paradigm provides a cover of scientific neutrality for policymakers and career opportunities for education scholars.

The purpose of this chapter is not to criticize policymakers or scholars; nor is it to denigrate our history of policymaking and educational research, some of which has been good for students who desperately need good things in their lives. Public education's record on many of these matters is good.

Both traditional and progressive educators, however, sense that some of the ways we govern, organize, and improve schools take us in the wrong direction. The purpose of this chapter is to agree with this "sense" and to expose the antieducational forces driving public education in this wrong direction. The first step toward improving public education is to reverse directions and start down a more promising path. What would that look like?

Our health care system is an example of a similarly integrated institution in need of reform. Comparing health care to public education illustrates that pursuing a new institutional direction means addressing the kinds of questions discussed thus far in chapters 1 and 2.

Our current health care system is based on the idea that private insurers can both provide good coverage and earn profits. For many years, this was possible because a high percentage of healthy people were paying insurance premiums through their employee benefit packages. Now that health insurance benefits are less common, health care is getting beyond the reach of the middle class, just as it has always been for the poor. We are now a society in which middle-income families without health insurance are one health crisis away from financial ruin.

Twenty years ago, nobody could have foreseen that thousands of manufacturing jobs, and the union contracts that provided health insurance, would become a thing of the past. Nobody could have foreseen such a rapid shift from a society in which middle-class families had health insurance to one in which they have to pay for it or go without it.

People who hope to improve our health care situation need to ask fundamental questions about what drives our current system. What are our beliefs about health care? Is high-quality health care a right or a privilege? What should the government's role be in providing health care? Medicare and Medicaid are already endangered by demographic factors and rising costs. Should they be reformed or eliminated in favor of different programs? Who benefits from our current system?

The first two chapters asked these same questions about American public education. What do we believe as a society? What is the current role of government? Who benefits from the existing system? Dissatisfaction with our current model's answers to these questions suggests that we should consider a completely new model. The next chapter presents such an alternative.

❸

THE ALTERNATIVE MODEL

The alternative model is different from our current model (shown in figure 1.1) in several ways.

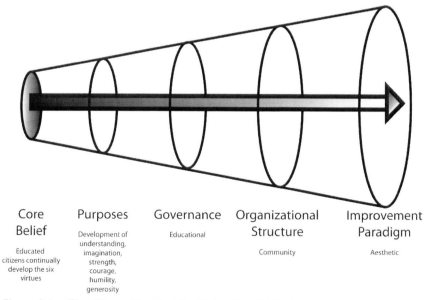

Core Belief	Purposes	Governance	Organizational Structure	Improvement Paradigm
Educated citizens continually develop the six virtues	Development of understanding, imagination, strength, courage, humility, generosity	Educational	Community	Aesthetic

Figure 3.1.   The Alternative Model of Schooling Neil Torda

First, the alternative model has an educational core belief instead of a political one. This is significant because a core belief drives the whole system. Just as a political core belief drives public education toward political purposes, an educational one drives it toward educational purposes.

Second, it reverses the order of the second and third elements. Within our current model, elected officials determine educational purposes, so governance is the second element and purpose is the third. This order is reversed in the alternative model so public education can serve the interests of students and families more than those of elected officials.

The third difference is that figure 3.1 has a focus that is absent from our current model. The single arrow represents the definition of what it means to be educated, and this definition enables public education to pursue purposes and govern in ways that are educational instead of political.

AN EDUCATIONAL CORE BELIEF
CHANGES EVERYTHING

The alternative core belief addresses the question of what it means to be educated. It defines educated persons as those who continually develop the virtues of *understanding, imagination, strong character, courage, humility,* and *generosity.* This means our uneducated human nature is characterized by the vices of ignorance, intellectual incompetence, weakness, fear, pride, and selfishness, which describes how humans come into the world. Becoming educated involves the struggle to overcome these vices by developing the virtues.

This definition does not contradict the desirability of democratic governance. It suggests a more fundamental premise—that the extent to which democratic governance is desirable is related to the extent to which the citizenry is educated. If citizens adopt this core belief, the purpose of public education will be focused on the development of students' minds, characters, and spirits. Isn't this the purpose of education?

PURPOSE PRECEDES GOVERNANCE

Since the middle of the 19th century, local school boards have governed public education in ways that achieve both public and private purposes. During the past 25 years, however, local control has been eroded as federal and state officials have identified public school purposes.

Graham (2005) described the shift this way:

> Throughout American history, our democratic society has required citizens to possess both virtue and knowledge, generally in that order of priority. Enthusiasm for *A Nation at Risk* reversed these priorities, primarily because many Americans feared that our economy was falling behind that of other nations whose citizens were more proficient academically than ours. (p. 161)

The stated purpose of today's public schools is to prepare students for employment in a competitive, global economy.

Educators grapple with two questions as they strive to achieve this purpose:

- What does it mean to prepare students for this kind of employment?
- How should this purpose be balanced with traditional ones?

The first question was the topic of "The Prepared Graduate" issue of *Educational Leadership* (April 2007). Scholars explained the need to prepare graduates to compete in a global economy. They argued for new curricula, new partnerships, new skill development, new organizational arrangements, new standards, and new assessments.

In the same issue, Schmoker (2007) discussed the second question. He argued for deepening a commitment to the traditional skills of reading, writing, and thinking.

Which is it? Should American public education be reformed to meet the demands of a global economy or should it better address traditional purposes?

When elected officials determine educational purposes, the answer depends on who is in power. Those with a stake in the economy point schools toward 21st-century purposes. Those who value our traditions point schools toward the knowledge and values of the past.

The motion of a pendulum is the perfect metaphor for our current model. Elected officials determine purposes, so education swings back and forth as it addresses the priorities of elected officials who have an orientation toward either the past or the future.

Figure 3.1 stops the pendulum by reversing the order of the second and third elements. In the alternative model, governance emerges from educational purposes. This raises a fundamental question: How are purposes established, if not through a democratic process that starts with electing policymakers at the local, state, and federal levels?

The alternative core belief answers this question. Its definition of the educated person provides a focus that is absent from today's system of public education. Unlike the diverging arrows of our current model, the alternative has a single arrow that represents the purpose of education, which is to build an educated citizenry. If we believe the educated person is one who develops the six virtues, the purposes of education are clear—to model and teach those virtues.

THE ALTERNATIVE MODEL'S EDUCATION FOCUS

The arrow in figure 3.1 focuses policymakers and school personnel as it passes through all the elements. When it comes to governance, policymakers must model the six virtues. They would be hypocritical to govern in ways that did not.

When it comes to organizational structure, the arrow focuses educators on forming school communities. No other organizational structure provides the environment in which young people develop these six virtues.

When it comes to school improvement, the alternative model requires an aesthetic paradigm. This means creative, imaginative school improvement approaches are valued over social scientific ones. Just as works of art express different perspectives on the human condition, school improvement efforts express different perspectives on the uneducated and educated human condition.

Simply put, because these specific virtues define the educated person, they are the focus of everything in the alternative model.

DEFINING THE SIX VIRTUES

In order to understand the significance of this focus, the six virtues need to be defined. The virtue meanings of strong character and generosity correspond to common usage, but the virtue meanings of understanding, imagination, courage, and humility do not. If we are to understand how the six virtues form our educated human nature, the meanings of all six need to be clear.

Educators mean different things by *understanding* and *imagination.* For example, Gardner (2000, p. 118) contrasts his definition of "understanding" with the cultural literacy definition, which defines it as knowing a lot of concepts and facts. Gardner (2000, p. 119), however, defines understanding as being able to apply knowledge to new situations: "An individual understands a concept, skill, theory, or domain of knowledge to the extent that he or she can apply it appropriately in a new situation."

The alternative model's virtue definition of understanding rests between the ideas of knowing facts and applying knowledge to new situations. The human mind works in two directions. Understanding is developed as the mind takes in sensory data and ideas. It is deepened as the mind uses new data to modify what it has already experienced and processed.

Human intellect also works in the other direction as it stimulates and directs behavior. What Gardner (2000) calls the application of understanding is what the alternative model calls the virtue of imagination. The mind takes in sensory data to develop understanding, and it expresses that understanding as it imagines new possibilities and actions.

Intellectual competence is the ability to act with imagination. People whose intellects are alive with new ideas and possibilities demonstrate the virtue meaning of imagination. They are intellectually competent because their imaginations enable them to take a broad range of actions. Sternberg (1996) called this "successful intelligence."

On the other hand, intellectually incompetent people are less able to act in new ways. They have less ability to use what they understand because they are less imaginative. As a result, they are less able to imagine a range of actions, less able to anticipate a range of consequences, and less able to direct their behavior accordingly.

For example, people who cannot make change at the cash register are intellectually incompetent because they are unable to use their understanding of addition and subtraction. Gardner (2000) says they lack understanding because they cannot apply what they understand. Sternberg (1996) says they lack "successful intelligence." The alternative model says they are intellectually incompetent.

Humans continually confront situations that require imagination, so this virtue is essential for improving the human condition. Unfortunately, the teaching of imagination in public schools is often relegated to the arts curriculum or is left to be developed on its own. The question for public educators is whether they do enough to promote imagination. Gardner (2000) and Sternberg (1996) use different language to ask the same question.

The virtue meaning of strong character is similar to its common use. It is the capacity to stand for what is right and good in the face of situations and desires that oppose what is right and good.

Public schools promote this virtue in several ways. The "hidden" curriculum requires students to do homework, meet deadlines, and be responsible. As students confront these requirements, they build character strength by increasing their capacity to delay gratification, cooperate with others, control impulses, engage in unpleasant activities, and accept responsibility.

Extracurricular programs also develop character strength. Students sacrifice and give extra effort when they commit to their teams, clubs, or fine arts activities. Their commitment builds strength as they challenge themselves to achieve high levels of performance.

The other character virtue is courage. One of the reasons its meaning is not clear is that it is not taught in public schools. Peck (1978, p. 131) provides a virtue definition of courage: "Courage is not the absence of fear; it is the making of action in spite of fear, the moving out against the resistance engendered by fear into the unknown and into the future." In this definition, the experience of fear is a call to action.

The emergence of virtuous action from a virtuous capacity is a key concept in the six-virtue definition of the educated person. In this case, the ability to act with courage emerges from a person's character strength capacity.

Palmer (1994) described how character strength is the capacity from which courageous actions emerge:

> The spiritual journey moves inward and downward. . . .
>
>   Why must we go in and down? Because as we do so, we will meet the violence and terror that we carry within ourselves. If we do not confront these things inwardly, we will project them outward onto other people. When we have not understood that the enemy is within ourselves, we will find a thousand ways of making someone "out there" into the enemy—people of a different race, a different sexual orientation. We will deal with our fears by killing the enemy, when what we really fear is the shadow within ourselves. (pp. 27–28)

Teaching courage begins with modeling and teaching the character strength that confronts the "violence and terror" within. This teaching is rare in public schools, but it need not be.

As a high school principal, I often dealt with students brought to the office for fighting. Usually these fights started with name-calling. I would ask the students to describe the insults they heard. Then I would ask: "Did calling you a 'bitch' (or other insult) make you a 'bitch?' Did calling you that name change you in any way?"

Students usually said the insults didn't change them. Building on this response, I would ask if they realized the insult reflected on the person using it, not on the one receiving it. On some occasions, the point sank in.

Most times, however, students were unwilling to look inside themselves to see that the fight was caused by the "violence and terror" within both the person hurling the insult and the person receiving it. Maybe this is because public schools teach fear instead of courage.

One way public educators teach fear is by modeling it themselves. They fear losing control of their classroom or school because they are outnumbered by students 20 to 1. Therefore, they create and enforce rules that teach students to be fearful too.

For example, many schools publish handbooks that detail the consequences for first, second, and third offenses. The purpose of this progressive disciplinary approach is to engender an ever-increasing fear of increasingly graver consequences. Is this the proper role for institutions of education? Where is the education in this approach?

What does it look like for public educators to model and teach courage, instead of fear? It starts with teachers taking the journey described by Palmer (1994). They must confront their fear of losing control. Then, instead of creating rules that teach students to be fearful, they must model and teach courage, instead of fear.

Teaching students to confront the code of silence that prevents them from "narcing" on their peers is an example of teaching courage. The frustrating thing about this code is that it masquerades as courage, even though it emerges from fear and is an expression of intellectual incompetence. It emerges from a fear of peer reprisal and it is intellectually incompetent because it fails to distinguish between prank behaviors and seriously destructive ones. Asking students to confront the code of silence provides the opportunity to teach them that real courage emerges from having the strength to confront the fear within themselves and to stand for what is right, even when peers don't agree.

I experienced this type of courage many years ago in a situation involving a sophomore girl and a junior boy. The boy was accused of vandalizing another student's artwork. As I interviewed students about the incident, none would violate the code. I mentioned the suspected boy by name, but none would tell what they knew.

As a veteran of public school administration, this did not surprise me. I was surprised, however, when a sophomore girl said she saw the accused boy vandalize the artwork and she was willing to say so in his presence. I remember her courage because it was a rarity during seven years of public high school administration.

Prior to this, I had many public school experiences in which teachers and parents defended the code of silence. They said we should not expect teenagers to "narc" on each other.

The opposite attitude prevails in parochial schools, where it is common for students to inform authorities of peer behaviors that damage the community. Parochial school communities rely on everyone to be courageous, so they model and teach it.

Courage can also be modeled and taught in public schools. The adults must do two things—overcome their own fear and teach that courage is righteous action that emerges from confronting the "violence and terror" within.

Generosity and humility are the spiritual virtue pair. Human spirits range from generous to selfish and from humble to proud.

The virtue definition of "generosity" coincides with its everyday use, so little needs to be explained here. Many public school educators model this virtue. They are drawn to service in public schools by their generous spirits, and this is modeled in their daily interactions with students.

My undergraduate students consistently report that they want to become teachers so they can give back to others. Similarly, my graduate students aspire to school administration because they want a career in which they serve teachers, parents, and students.

Of course, not all public school educators are generous, and generosity is not the norm in all schools. But educators who lack generosity are unhappy in their careers, and schools where generosity is not the norm are dysfunctional.

For the most part, school personnel model and teach the generosity that makes schools functional. The modeling of teachers and principals provides young people with many opportunities to experience the beauty of a generous spirit.

This is not the case with humility. Modern society has not resolved the contradiction between its philosophical and popular meanings, so we don't recognize the virtue meaning of humility.

Dictionaries feed the confusion as they define pride in positive ways. Modern meanings of pride suggest that it is a virtue, instead of a vice, so educators and parents tell students they are proud of them, and they want students to be proud of their accomplishments.

The writings of many Christian philosophers, however, describe pride as the first of the seven deadly sins. Therefore, shouldn't we be humbled by our children's achievements, and shouldn't we want children to be humble in accomplishment?

Apparently not—dictionaries define humility as an undesirable quality. Today's notions of humility associate it with weakness and low ability.

But this makes no sense. Jesus was a model of humility not because he was lowly, but because he was exalted. Humility is not a quality of those who lack talent. If a person is not good at something, it is not humility to believe so. It is reality. Humility starts with knowing one is good. Only those with true gifts and talents can demonstrate humility.

At the same time humble people know they are good, they realize others care little about their goodness. They don't brag because, in the face of the indifference of others, bragging would make them fools. Furthermore, secure in the knowledge of their goodness, they don't need a spotlight on their abilities. This enables humble people to recognize and shine a light on the achievements of others.

Finally, humble people know that, the day after they die, the world goes on just as it did the day before. All the great accomplishments imaginable do not alter this fact.

The philosophical meaning of humility is that it is a virtue displayed by those who know they are good, know others care little about their goodness, recognize the talents of others, and understand their insignificance in the big scheme of things.

Unfortunately, modern meanings denigrate humility and regard pride as a virtuous sense of worth. Although pride may not harm others, its self-satisfying nature tends to prevent improvement. I recently experienced this effect as I was reading student evaluations of one of my graduate courses.

Several wrote that the class helped them think more clearly about education. They gained new insights, and they understood things more deeply. As I read their comments, I felt a sense of pride welling up inside. With each comment, my image of myself grew more appealing. Here was evidence that I was a good professor. I was feeling proud of myself, and I was feeling no need to improve.

Then cynicism grabbed me. I wondered if my students were praising me because this was a professional norm. Were their comments little more than the positive attitudes educators were supposed to express?

But I am not that cynical, so I kept trying to understand the meaning of what they had written. Suddenly a humbling sensation washed over me. It was as though the curtains had been drawn, and I could see the students hunched over their evaluation forms, writing about that semester's experience.

After the curtains of pride and cynicism were drawn, I could see that the students were describing our shared experience. Only then could I see the beauty of what they had written. Their comments were less about my teaching than they were about their own efforts, their own learning, and their own development. I was reading about them, not me. After pride was pushed aside, I could find the humility to see that the great achievements of that semester were theirs.

That is why the alternative model uses the philosophical meanings of pride and humility. Humility is a virtue that shines a light on others and makes growth and improvement possible. Pride is self-satisfaction that seeks the light and, by doing so, casts a shadow on others.

THE VIRTUES RELATE TO EACH OTHER IN SEVERAL WAYS

Relationships among the six virtues help clarify their meanings and significance. They are three pairs that address three aspects of human development.

The first of each pair is a capacity developed through education and experience. The second is an ability that emerges from the first. In Comte-Sponville's (2001, p. 1) words, each of the virtue pairs addresses "what we should do, what we should be, and how we should live."

For example, our capacity to understand enables us to take actions that are more or less imaginative. As understanding deepens, more possibilities can be imagined and acted upon.

Similarly, character strength is the capacity that enables courageous action. Just as athletes build muscle strength to enable higher levels of performance, citizens who build strong character are more able to act with courage in difficult situations.

Consider situations where citizens risk their lives to rescue someone in immediate danger. When others want to call them courageous, they often deny that they are "heroes" because their behavior emerged more from the need to take immediate action than from inner strength.

On the other hand, when soldiers act to save the lives of endangered comrades, their actions are courageous because they emerge from the character strength built from the first day of enlistment. Courageous action in battle emerges from a well of strength that begins in boot camp.

The point is that people who put themselves in danger are not necessarily courageous. The presence of danger does not make an act courageous. Putting one's self in danger is courageous when it emerges from strong character.

The spiritual virtues relate to each other in the same way. The epilogue explains more about how humility is the capacity that makes generosity virtuous.

The third way the virtues relate to each other is that they are completely interconnected. They can be separated in discussion but not in human behavior or situations. All human behavior is an expression of the combined six virtues and six vices within all of us.

Aristotle's principle of the Golden Mean is helpful here. It argues that extremes should be avoided, even extremes of virtue. Therefore, Aristotle placed virtues at the midpoint of a continuum. An example is that the virtue of gentleness is the midpoint between indifference and irascibility (Sahakian, 1968, p. 74). When virtues are considered separately, extremes should be avoided and the Golden Mean makes sense.

But this conclusion assumes virtue exists on a continuum, which ignores the complexity of life. The alternative model embraces the complexity of life by assuming virtues and vices are always interrelated to each other in all human behavior. Individuals react to different situations with behavior that is more or less virtuous. Behavior emerges from mixtures of our capacities and our ability to behave in ways that are either virtuous or vicious.

An example of this interrelatedness is how a state legislature funds public education. In states that provide poor children with equal educational opportunities, the legislators demonstrate understanding, imagination, and generosity. They *understand* it is bad policy for poor children to become members of a permanent underclass. Therefore, they *imagine* ways to equalize funding that are acceptable to taxpayers in wealthy districts. And their *generosity* gives poor children the same opportunities they want for their own.

In many states, however, children of the poor are not provided equal educational opportunities. In these states, legislators may *understand* that it is bad policy to leave poor children behind, but *intellectual incompetence* prevents them from equalizing funding in acceptable ways. *Fear* prevents them from proposing legislation that jeopardizes reelection. And *pride* credits them with having good intentions as poor children are disadvantaged by the status quo. They may talk about providing equal educational opportunities, but they lack the combination of virtues needed to make it happen.

In a column published in the *Asheville Citizen-Times*, I explained that North Carolina school funding laws sponsor educational inequalities throughout the state. Shortly after this column appeared, a state legislator spoke to my politics of education class. After his presentation, I walked him to the door and handed him a copy of my column entitled "Inequality of School Funding Should Shame N.C. Legislators" (Hurley, 2005). I have not heard from him since.

If I conclude that he did not read the column, I wonder if he is developing an understanding of his primary legislative responsibility, which is to provide equal educational opportunity for all North Carolina children. If I conclude that he read it and chose not to respond, I wonder if he is developing the imagination, strength, and courage needed to sponsor legislation that would end North Carolina's discrimination against poor children. I suppose this is a safe assumption. He has good intentions. Without the virtues of imagination, character strength, and courage, however, good intentions do not improve the education of North Carolina's poor children.

The alternative model assumes virtues and vices cannot be separated in human situations, so it avoids Aristotle's concern about extremes. The human condition is made better by educated citizens who demonstrate the six virtues. The more educated the person, the more virtuous the behavior, and the better the human condition.

GOVERNING EDUCATIONALLY

When I tell graduate students that education should be governed educationally, not politically, they are quick to reply, "Politics drives everything in education. You can't change that."

Golden (2004) described this kind of belief as the "inevitability trap":

> Near as I can tell, it starts when the people who will benefit from these choices simply begin to assert their inevitability. . . . So the myth of inevitability spreads and the prophecy fulfills itself. If the proponents of a particular course can get a critical mass of folks to believe that it's a foregone conclusion, pretty soon it will be. (p. 344)

It is time to confront the inevitability trap of believing public education must be governed politically.

Why shouldn't education be governed educationally? Other institutions are governed in ways that align with their purposes. Business is governed by rules of the marketplace. The legal system is governed by legislation and court decisions. Religion is governed by sacred texts and the interpretations of those ordained to preach. Why can't public education be governed in a way that models what it means to be educated?

It can be, when our model is driven by a core belief that is educational and when our model is one in which purpose precedes governance. The alternative model changes our current model in these two ways. Instead of being driven by a political core belief that assumes we will always be in debate over purposes, the alternative model is driven by a universal definition of what it means to be educated.

The next chapter explains the universality of this definition. For now, readers should challenge the trap that says public education must be governed democratically. Democracy does not require us to believe in either its desirability or its inevitability. Instead, it requires that citizens be educated enough to sustain it. The next chapter explains how the six-virtue definition guides us toward that end.

4

CORE BELIEFS DRIVE EDUCATION

A core belief is the first element in both models. According to De Pree (1989, p. 24), "What we believe precedes policy and practice."

This chapter begins with a definition of core beliefs. Then it describes how American public schools are driven by a political core belief and how parochial schools are driven by religious ones. The third section describes the core belief of the alternative model. The fourth section argues that schools should be driven by a definition of what it means to be educated. And the last section describes barriers to adopting the six-virtue definition of what it means to be educated.

WHAT IS A CORE BELIEF?

Core beliefs have three qualities that distinguish them from other beliefs:

- They are rooted in a society's traditions and history.
- They are rarely discussed or debated.
- The opposite belief is rejected outright. A test for core-belief status is to ask how a society would regard its opposite.

Because core beliefs are deeply rooted and rarely discussed, they can be invisible to cultural insiders. Sometimes they are more easily identified by cultural outsiders who gain extensive knowledge of a society. My work with Jamaican educators has provided me with the opportunity to develop such knowledge. I have taught more than 30 Western Carolina University courses all over Jamaica, which is the third-largest English-speaking culture in the Western Hemisphere. Only the United States and Canada are larger. All three societies trace their origins to the European settlement of the Americas. Unlike the United States and Canada, however, Jamaican traditions are rooted in slavery and shaped by British colonialism.

Concerning core beliefs, Jamaicans and Americans share the belief that public education provides students with an opportunity for upward social and economic mobility. Therefore, both invest heavily in public education.

One difference between the two belief systems is that Jamaicans do not share the American reverence for democracy. The first time I taught in Jamaica was during their 1990 parish elections. When students objected to having class on Election Day, I assumed this was an expression of their reverence for the democratic process. I was wrong.

They objected because travel would not be safe that day. During the 1970s and 1980s, election days in Kingston had turned violent, as members of both political parties took to the streets to prevent rivals from voting.

Furthermore, during the 1970s, Jamaica established economic and diplomatic relations with the Soviet Union and Cuba. Both of these historical events are examples of how the Jamaican experience with democracy is different from ours.

If Jamaicans do not share our core belief, what drives their system of public education? I have asked my Jamaican classes this question on several occasions.

Each time we discussed their history, traditions, and culture to explore various possibilities. Eventually we concluded that Jamaica's educational core belief is that elected and appointed authorities are responsible for citizen welfare. We can evaluate this idea for core-belief status by asking if it is rooted in their traditions and history, if it is rarely debated, and if the opposite belief is largely rejected by Jamaicans.

A belief in the power of authorities is deeply rooted in Jamaican culture. It was promoted by British slave owners and reinforced during colonial rule.

And this belief is rarely debated. Every day, Jamaicans call in to radio talk shows to demand that elected officials take certain actions. As a cultural outsider, it sounds to me like the purpose of these programs is to lecture Jamaican authorities. Sometimes the talk show host suggests that ordinary citizens also have a role to play in addressing their concerns. This idea hangs in the airwaves until the next caller demands that authorities take some other action.

When asked how Jamaicans would regard the opposite belief, my students say they could not argue that ordinary citizens are responsible for improving the general welfare. In their minds, it is clear that the authorities are responsible for this. Furthermore, just like within our current model of American public education, modeling and teaching this core belief drives much of Jamaican education.

One of my Jamaican friends is a school board member. He recently heard so many complaints about the school's principal that he met informally with some of the teachers. After listening to their complaints, he asked in frustration, "Do you really think all these problems would be solved by hiring a new principal?" The response was a resounding, "Yes."

Jamaican independence from England has meant that colonial rulers (and slave masters before them) have been replaced by elected officials and their appointees. It may be ironic, or it may be cause and effect, that Bob Marley was an eloquent voice for citizen power in a society that believes so much in citizen powerlessness.

The same questions can be asked to determine if the desirability of democratic governance is an American core belief. Does it emerge from our history and traditions? Is it taken for granted and rarely debated? How would Americans respond to the opposite belief?

The desirability of democratic governance is deeply rooted in our traditions and history. Our country was founded in the 18th century so free men could govern themselves. Lincoln's 19th-century description of a "government of the people, by the people, and for the people" reinforced our belief in democracy, and continues to inspire us today.

Dewey (1938) described the sources of this belief:

> We have been taught not only in the schools but by the press, the pulpit, the platform, and our laws and law-making bodies, that democracy is the best of all social institutions. We may have so assimilated this idea from our surroundings that it has become an habitual part of our mental and moral make-up. (p. 34)

The desirability of democratic governance is deeply rooted in our traditions.

Our efforts to establish a democratic government in Iraq reflect the strength of this belief. We sincerely believe Iraqis should govern themselves democratically, even though they live in a different part of the world, their history is nothing like ours, and their culture has different traditions and values. This belief was never debated, and to this day it is unquestioningly shared among the vast majority of Americans.

Finally, what do Americans say about opposite beliefs? How do we respond to the belief that democracy is not a desirable form of government? How do we respond to the belief that other forms of government are more desirable than democracy? Both beliefs are rejected outright by the vast majority of Americans.

HOW DOES THIS CORE BELIEF DRIVE PUBLIC EDUCATION?

Americans believe in the desirability of democratic governance, but the question remains: How does this belief drive public education? The first way is obvious. Because of this belief, elected officials at the local and state levels represent citizens in the governance of public education.

Chapter 2 described a second reason to claim our belief in the desirability of democratic governance drives public education. This belief, combined with the principle that federal governance supercedes state governance, which supercedes local governance; explains why so few, educators and elected officials objected to NCLB's intrusion into public education. The law provides few benefits, but it comes at a great cost to teachers' options for addressing students' individual needs. Still, local and state objections to this intrusion have only been that it was not fully funded by the federal government.

We have a dysfunctional situation created by our core belief in the desirability of democratic governance. American school purposes are unbalanced because federal officials in the executive and legislative branches, who are not elected to govern education are asserting authority over the local and state policymakers who are elected to govern education.

This dysfunction and imbalance has resulted in educational purposes that are more political than educational. These political purposes were accomplished in three steps.

First, educational achievement became synonymous with standardized test scores. Elected officials forced this definition on the public, even though it is a shallow view of what public educators try to accomplish with students.

Second, this definition prompted the expansion of the standardized test industry. This expense was approved by elected officials who vowed to hold teachers accountable. This idea does little to improve student learning, which is infinitely more complex than what standardized tests measure, as it drains resources that could be spent on achieving deeper, more important purposes.

The third step was to reward and sanction schools on the basis of student test scores. Elected officials score political points by claiming to hold educators accountable for higher tests scores, but this idea ignores the investment needed to improve education for children in the worst schools.

Politically motivated elected officials have focused public education on improving standardized test scores, simply because this is a purpose for which educators can be held accountable. It does not matter that this is a shallow purpose. It only matters that incumbents can use it to appeal to voters.

A second example of how educational purposes are subordinated to political ones is the failure of state legislatures to provide equitable funding (Biddle & Berliner, 2002; Germeraad, 2008). Since 1960, more than 40 states have been sued for failing to equitably fund the educations of children living in property-poor school districts. If educational purposes were primary, state legislators would insist on providing equal educational opportunities for the children most in need of public education.

The distinction between political and educational purposes is no small matter. The importance of having educational purposes for schools can be seen by comparing public school political purposes with parochial school religious purposes. Both religious and political purposes are often barriers to educational ones.

For example, Pope Benedict XVI's declaration that "Catholicism provides the only true path to salvation" (Winfield, 2007), expresses a religious purpose for America's largest system of parochial education. Morris-Young (2007, pp. 1, 7) clarified the educational intent of this declaration: "The recent Vatican document emphasizing that only the Catholic Church possesses the fullness of the means for salvation was created primarily as an instructional tool for Catholics and should not be read as a diminishing of other faith communities." In other words, the pope's belief statement is meant to guide Catholic educators. On careful examination, however, this statement is antieducational because it promotes and demonstrates the vices of intellectual incompetence, fear, and pride.

The antieducational nature of the pope's statement becomes evident when contrasted with Moore's (2000) reflection on his Catholicism:

> I expect to be Catholic all my life. . . . I hope to learn continually from every possible spiritual tradition in the world, deepening my Catholicism and my humanity at the same time. . . . I have much to learn from everyone I meet who is also openly approaching the mysteries that make us human and allow us to live together in a world that needs our participation. (pp. 312–313)

Moore's statement, unlike the pope's, demonstrates and promotes the virtues of understanding, humility, imagination, and generosity.

History tells of the results we get when political and religious beliefs drive education. It is so full of stories about war that many believe it is our human nature to war against each other.

The alternative model sees it differently. It distinguishes between our uneducated human nature and our educated one. This distinction offers the hope that a virtue definition of what it means to be educated can drive educational systems that prepare citizens to live in peace with one another, just as political and religious beliefs drive us to war with each other. That is why the alternative model replaces political and religious core beliefs with a universal, six-virtue definition of what it means to be educated.

WHY THESE SIX VIRTUES AND NOT OTHERS?

Why is the educated person one who develops understanding, imagination, strong character, courage, humility, and generosity? Why not respect, cooperation, honesty, perseverance, or other equally desirable virtues? To answer these questions and to examine the universality of this definition, four questions are addressed in this section:

- Is the list of six virtues conceptually consistent?

- Is it fundamental?
- Is it comprehensive?
- Is it concise enough to be educationally useful?

Comte-Sponville (2001) reduced his virtue list from 30 to 18 by eliminating overlap. He wrote that he eliminated virtues that are "covered" by others. For example, he discarded kindness because it is covered by generosity. The six-virtue list avoids overlap, too.

An example of a conceptually inconsistent list is the character education curriculum that teaches the 10 traits "most commonly named by parents, educators, and community groups concerned with character education" (Elkind & Sweet, 2007a). The ten traits are trustworthiness, respect, responsibility, fairness, caring, citizenship, honesty, courage, diligence, and integrity.

This list is conceptually inconsistent in two ways. First, it lists trustworthiness, honesty, and integrity as equals, but the first two are parts of the third. In other words, it does not avoid overlap. Second, nine of the qualities are nouns, but "caring" is an adjective.

The six virtues of the educated person do not overlap because they are the most fundamental of the intellectual, character, and spiritual virtues. This premise can be tested by comparing these six with the virtues in other lists. For example, Comte-Sponville (2001) puts "compassion" on his list of 18 virtues. Is "compassion" a fundamental virtue, or does it emerge from some combination of the six virtues?

A compassionate person *understands* the difficulty of another's situation and *imagines* what the other person feels. Furthermore, compassion is expressed in *imaginative* and *generous* acts that emerge from a person's *understanding* and *humility*.

Expressions of compassion are expressions of a combination of these four more fundamental virtues. An analogous situation is a cake recipe. A cake does not exist without the ingredients; but, because the ingredients can exist without being a cake, the ingredients are the more fundamental elements. In the same way, the six virtues are the ingredients of other virtues.

Humor is another virtue in Comte-Sponville's (2001) list of 18 virtues. In order to produce humor, a comedian must *understand* an audience and deliver a punch line that prompts audience members to use their imaginations to fill in the funny part. Humor does not exist without *understanding* and *imagination*, but *understanding* and *imagination* can exist without humor.

Trustworthiness is one of the 10 "In Search of Character" traits (Elkind & Sweet, 2007a). It, too, is formed from two of the six more fundamental virtues. Trustworthiness is not a virtue unless it emerges from *strong character* and *courage*. An example is the code of trust expressed by members of the Mafia or the Ku Klux Klan. They may live according to this code, but their trust lacks virtue because it emerges from weakness and fear, not from a strong character that "meets the violence and terror" within (Palmer, 1994).

Responsibility is another trait that emerges from two more fundamental virtues. Responsible actions are virtuous when they emerge from both *understanding* and *strong character*.

For example, the female lead in the high school musical may responsibly carry out her extracurricular duties, but virtuousness is compromised if she does not *understand* that schoolwork is her first priority, or if she does not have the *character strength* to keep homework as a priority during rehearsal season. Responsible musical performers are virtuous when they have the understanding and strong character to keep schoolwork as their first responsibility.

Morris's (1997) list of 52 virtues is another virtue set that can be compared to the six virtues of the educated person. For example, is cooperativeness (Morris, 1997) a virtue? It often is, but not when people cooperate as a way to get what they want for themselves. In these cases, cooperation is not a virtue because it lacks the *humility* and *generosity* that make cooperation a virtue. In other words, Morris' list includes virtue behaviors that are sometimes not virtuous, like the trustworthiness example from the "In Search of Character" traits (Elkind & Sweet, 2007a).

Cheerfulness is another virtue on Morris's (1997) list. Cheerfulness is not a virtue when it is expressed by the person who wins the lottery, but it is a virtue when expressed by the neighbor of the person who wins the lottery. In this example cheerfulness is a virtue because it is expressed with a spirit of *generosity* that *imagines* another's good fortune.

Space does not allow discussing all of Morris's (1997) virtues, but the result is always the same. Each of them emerges from combinations of the six fundamental virtues.

In summary, the six-virtue list is conceptually consistent because it avoids overlap, all its virtues take noun forms, and it includes just the most fundamental of virtues.

The six-virtue definition of the educated person is also comprehensive because it covers what distinguishes humans from other animals. Comte-Sponville (2001, p. 4) explained that his 18 virtues describe "dispositions of heart, mind, or character" because these aspects of our humanity distinguish us from other animals. For the same reason, the alternative core belief defines the educated person as one who develops intellect, character, and spirit. Those who develop these aspects of their nature become more human and less like other animals.

Second, as mentioned in chapter 3, Comte-Sponville (2001, p. 1) explained that virtues address both what we should be and do. The six virtues are three pairs in which one is a capacity and the other is an ability to act. The more fully developed our understanding, the more potential we have for imaginative thinking. The same is true for the strong character that enables courageous action, and for the humility that makes generosity a virtue.

Third, chapter 3 also mentioned that the six virtues and their opposite vices can be separated in discussion, but not in human behavior or situations. Whether human behavior in any situation is educated or uneducated depends on how it expresses combinations of the six virtues and six vices.

For example, when I was a boy, my parents wanted me to be patient in the doctor's waiting room. They said the doctor would see me as soon as possible, but he was busy with other patients.

As an adult, I still wait for long periods in doctors' waiting rooms, but now I realize it is because doctors take it literally when they schedule "patients." I have to wait because doctors schedule their days so they don't have to wait for patients, even if that means patients have to wait long periods for them. A professional norm for doctors is that their time is more important than that of their patients.

My adult patience is of a different quality than my boyhood patience. Some might say it emerges from understanding and imagination enriched by years of experience in waiting rooms. They would be right.

Others might say it emerges from a pride that is offended every time I have to wait for doctors who believe their time is more important than mine. They would be right, too. Although my adult patience is informed by years of experience and understanding, it is just as uneducated as my boyhood patience because it expresses more pride than humility.

Any virtue list that aspires to teach young people how to become educated requires an approach comprehensive enough to deal with the complexities of human life. The alternative model's core belief acknowledges this complexity by recognizing that all human behavior emerges from combinations of our virtuous capacities and abilities as we struggle to overcome the vices of our uneducated nature.

Can a virtue list that defines what it means to be educated, and that addresses the complexities of human life provide a clear, educational focus? Many virtue lists are too long. Philosophers get carried away when they start identifying human virtues. Morris's (1997) list of 52 is a good example. So is Comte-Sponville's (2001) list of 18. The six-virtue list, however, is short enough to provide a focus for what policymakers and school personnel can model and teach.

Long lists of virtues make it difficult to know which ones to model in which situations. The list of three virtue pairs, however, means that understanding is the intellectual *capacity* that always needs to be modeled and imagination is always a desired intellectual *capability*. Strength of character is the character capacity that always needs to be modeled, and courage is always a desired character capability. Humility is the spiritual capacity that always needs to be modeled, and generosity is always a desired spiritual capability.

Modeling virtue is more important than teaching it, anyway. The first sentence of Comte-Sponville's (2001, p. 1) treatise states, "If virtue can be taught, as I believe it can, it is not through books so much as by example." If the only thing that changed in public schools were that policymakers and school personnel modeled the six virtues, public education would be vastly improved.

Not only is the list of six virtues short enough to provide an educational focus, but public schools already teach three of them (understanding, character strength, and generosity). Adding imagination, courage, and humility sharpens the educational value of all six. Young people should learn that understanding gives pleasure when it sparks imagination, that character strength makes courageous action possible, and that virtuous generosity emerges from humility.

WHY DON'T WE TEACH SIX VIRTUES?

So why isn't the educated person defined as one who develops all six virtues? The next section discusses the barriers to adopting this core belief.

A core belief that focuses public education on teaching virtue encounters several barriers. The first is that too many philosophical discussions of virtue use outdated language. For example, the Greek cardinal virtues of justice, prudence, fortitude, and temperance are less relevant today than the virtues of critical thinking, insight, and persuasiveness. If public education is going to be driven by the teaching of virtue, its language must be modern.

A second more substantial barrier is that virtues are often associated with religious teachings. Citizens who are wary of religion in public schools might be alarmed by the suggestion that the purpose of public education is to teach six virtues. A connection between religion and virtue is strong in people's minds, even though it need not be.

Third, policymakers and school personnel are likely to prefer the current model because it requires them to model and teach only the same three virtues that were modeled and taught to them (understanding, strong character, and generosity). Policymakers and educators do not value imagination, courage, and humility because they, themselves, learned to be intellectually incompetent, fearful, and proud.

Here is Dyer's (1976) description of what students learn in public schools:

> When you left home and arrived in school, you entered an institution that is designed expressly to instill approval-seeking thinking and behavior. Ask permission to do everything. Never bank on your own judgment. Ask the teacher to go to the bathroom. Sit in a particular seat. Don't leave it under penalty of a demerit. Everything was geared toward other-control. Instead of learning to think you were being taught not to think for yourself. Fold your paper into sixteen squares, and don't write on the folds. Study chapters one and two tonight. Practice these words in spelling. Draw like this. Read that. You were taught to be obedient. And if in doubt, check it out with the teacher. If you should incur the teacher's, or worse yet, the principal's wrath, you were expected to feel guilty for months. Your report card was a message to your parents telling them how much approval you had won. . . .
>
> Any student who shows signs of self-actualization and personal mastery is quickly put in his place. Students who are independent, full of self-love, not susceptible to guilt and worry, are systematically labeled troublemakers.
>
> Schools are not good at dealing with kids who show signs of independent thinking. In too many schools approval-seeking is the way to success. The old cliché of teacher's pet and apple polishing are clichés for a reason. They exist—and work. If you gain the acclamation of the staff, behave in the ways that they dictate, study the curriculum that is laid out in front of you, you'll emerge successful. Albeit with a strong *need* for approval, since self-reliance has been discouraged at virtually every turn. (pp. 56–57)

Dyer (1976) believes schools teach "approval-seeking" behavior, but I give public education slightly more credit.

My experience is that public school personnel teach understanding that is intellectually incompetent, strong character that is fearful, and generosity that is proud. This gets modeled and taught from generation to generation because educators are unlikely to value the virtues that were ignored in their own educations.

Fourth, policymakers and school personnel believe it is more important to make and enforce rules than it is to model and teach six virtues. Public schools have rules for everything. They even have rules about the enforcement of rules. School boards and state legislatures have recently adopted zero-tolerance policies, which means the judgment of educators is replaced by a rule enforcing a rule.

The distinction between a virtue-based approach to education and a rules-based one is evident in how attendance policies are enforced differently in Catholic schools and public schools. Catholic educators regard the enforcement of class attendance policies as an occasion to teach virtue.

As a Catholic school student, I learned that skipping class was an affront to the dedication of the teachers. All students were expected to *understand* their teachers' dedication, *imagine* the insulting message sent by skipping class, have the *character strength* to attend class when they did not feel like it, and have the *courage* to go against the peer pressure that encourages skipping.

On the other hand, as a public high school administrator, I enforced attendance policies by teaching about the rules in the student handbook. The closest I came to teaching virtue was when I taught students to *understand* the attendance policy and the consequences for violating it.

The reasons students should not skip class are the same in both parochial and public schools. These two types of schools differ greatly, however, in what they teach about the importance of attending class. Parochial schools teach why it is virtuous to attend class, public schools teach that truant students get detention.

Lacking a foundation in the teaching of agreed-upon virtues, public school rules continually expand in number. Public schools have rules that govern all aspects of school life, just like in the larger society.

Other societies, however, sometimes take a virtue-based approach to life. An example is driving in Kingston, Jamaica, during rush-hour traffic.

Whenever taxi drivers take me to class during the afternoon rush hour, they creep out of the hotel driveway—deliberately in front of a car that has the right-of-way. I always expect to see an angry driver in the other car, but I never do. They always respond by signaling my driver to cut in line.

When Kingston drivers respond this way, they demonstrate several virtues. They *understand* the plight of another driver trying to get into traffic, they *imagine* they could be in the same position, they are *generous* as they decide the other person's needs are worthy, and their *humility* is evident in a willingness to let someone in line whose needs may not be greater than their own.

Why do they do this? One reason is that they have to use a virtue-based system. The Jamaican government lacks the funds needed to install more traffic signs, lights, and other regulating equipment. When drivers let another car in line, they are part of a system that lets them in line when they have the same need. This system is a beautiful thing to experience, especially when compared to the ugliness of driving in American cities.

All four barriers to teaching virtue are overcome in the list of six virtues. They are expressed in modern language, they are unrelated to religious teaching, they are not burdensome because they are an extension of the three virtues already taught in public schools, and public schools could take a virtue-based approach instead of a rules-based one, if they so chose. Many parochial schools take a virtue-based approach, which often attracts parents to these institutions. Public schools would be vastly improved if they realized that every educational institution's most important purpose is to teach virtue. When that purpose is achieved, society has less need for rules.

CONCLUSION

Core beliefs drive education. Today's public schools are driven by a political core belief, and parochial schools are driven by religious ones. What would it look like for an education system to be driven by an educational core belief?

This chapter addressed this question by describing a core belief that is based on a six-virtue definition of what it means to be educated. Humans are different from other animals by virtue of our intellectual, character, and spiritual capacities and capabilities.

The six-virtue definition of the educated person is the core belief that drives the alternative model. It is conceptually consistent, comprehensive, and concise enough to guide policymakers and school personnel. We need an educational system driven by a definition of what it means to be educated simply because the purpose of education is to produce educated people. Human history demonstrates that political and religious core beliefs drive us to war against each other. The alternative model's core belief points schools toward producing educated people who are capable of living in peace with each other.

We turn now to the educational purposes of the alternative model. Of course, these are to model and teach the six virtues.

5

VIRTUE-BASED
EDUCATIONAL PURPOSES

As I picked up the *Educational Leadership* issue entitled "Educating the Whole Child" (May 2007), I sarcastically muttered, "Now we are supposed to educate the whole child? What were we doing before— educating their fingers, or maybe just their toes?" Then I realized public schools are so focused on standardized tests scores that, in fact, they no longer educate the whole child.

The idea of holding educators accountable for student performance on standardized tests has narrowed the purposes of public education so much that the Association for Supervision and Curriculum Development (ASCD) has started an initiative called "The Whole Child." This is both a good idea and a sign that something has gone terribly wrong.

ASCD and many public educators are finally pushing back against more than 20 years of focusing on standardized test scores. Pushing against this idea would make more sense, however, if public educators also pushed toward something. What should that be? Educating the whole child is not the answer. It makes us look silly. Of course we educate the whole child. Nobody has ever proposed not to.

The alternative model suggests that the purpose of public education should be to model and teach the six virtues of the educated person. Although this is not what ASCD meant by educating the whole child, it could be. Public schools already model and teach understanding, strong character, and generosity. The alternative model simply adds imagination, courage, and humility.

In all models of education, purposes are the foundation for debates about curriculum and the type of future for which young people should be prepared. The following sections describe these purposes and debates across several models of education.

THE STANDARDS AND ACCOUNTABILITY MODEL

Figure 5.1 illustrates one set of purposes, along with a debate about curriculum and a vision of the future. Our current purposes are listed in the base of the circle because they are the foundation for the curricular debate, which is in the middle band. The vision of the future is at the top.

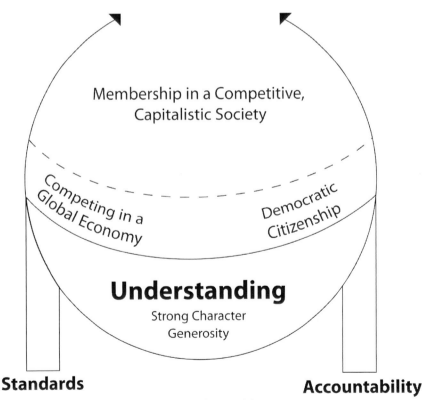

Figure 5.1. Preparing for Capitalistic Competition Neil Torda

The standards and accountability movement of the 1990s is based on the assumption that students learn more when educators are held accountable for achieving the standards established by state and federal legislators. Policymakers have established the improvement of student test scores as not only the dominant purpose of public education but also its only purpose, because these are measures for which school personnel can be held accountable.

This emphasis is depicted in the bold typeface of *Understanding*. This is also depicted in the standards and accountability pillars, which hold the base steady. Teachers no longer address the varying needs of individual students because the standards and accountability movement judges all educators on the basis of student test scores.

The pillars of standards and accountability explain why ASCD's "The Whole Child" initiative gets little attention in schools. Teachers and principals actually educate the whole child, but policymakers cannot hold them accountable for that, so they have become focused on improving student test scores. Most understand this is what they are supposed to do, as told to them by their bureaucratic superiors—so they do it.

The middle band of figure 5.1 depicts a curriculum debate about the need to prepare students for competition in a global economy versus the need to prepare them for democratic citizenship. North Carolina and West Virginia, for example, have developed curricula emphasizing the first purpose.

The top part of the circle identifies a vision of the future for which students are being prepared. A vision of America in competition with other capitalistic societies replaces the Cold War vision that dominated before the fall of the Soviet Union.

According to Armstrong (2006), these purposes, this curricular debate, and this vision of the future is the "Academic Achievement Discourse" that dominates today's discussions of how to improve education.

This discourse was evident in Michelle Rhee's C-Span interview with Brian Lamb (Rhee, 2007), shortly after she was named chancellor of the Washington, D.C., public schools. Five times she said holding employees accountable was her main function. For example, she said:

> I think in the next few weeks as I'm sitting down with every single one
> of the principals, it's going to be a different conversation, because we're

going to sit down and we're going to look at the data. Our test score data just came back, so I have a very clear view into how the students at each one of our schools is performing. And we're going to talk with the data as an anchor. And then I am going to listen to them about what they think, again, they can deliver.

One reason standards and accountability dominate public education discourse is that senior administrators believe holding subordinates accountable for higher test scores is their main function.

Those who see student achievement in more complex ways realize that holding educators accountable may or may not improve it. Reason and experience tell them that holding educators accountable sometimes improves achievement, sometimes has no effect, and sometimes has negative effects.

This is the same point made by those who argue that higher levels of funding do not necessarily improve student achievement. Of course that is true, just as it is true that holding educators accountable does not necessarily improve student achievement.

The story of a Northeastern alternative high school is an example. Since the 1960s, the Durant School (a pseudonym) had a history of being an excellent alternative high school (Goodson & Foote, 2001). In 1997 it sought exemption from the state accountability testing program because standardized tests were antithetical to its mission. According to Goodson and Foote (2001):

> It was in April that year (1996) that the state's commissioner of education announced the adoption of a series of five standardized exams—in five different content areas—to measure the attainment of the state's new higher standards by high school students. The passage of all five exams would be mandatory for graduation, and no public high school student would be exempt.

The school's request to be exempt from this requirement was denied several times.

It did not matter that Durant School adults and students demonstrated their commitment to democratic purposes by organizing, lobbying, and being a community. And it did not matter that

the city's mayor recently commented on the school's achievements in a letter to the state education commissioner, noting that the school's "success
rate in graduating at-risk students is approximately 20 percent higher than
the City School District's average rate." In addition, the school "boasts
some of the District's highest attendance rates, highest SAT scores, lowest suspension rates, and lowest dropout rates." The mayor concluded
that this school's "non-traditional, yet rigorous process for demanding
accountability and assessing knowledge serves its students well" [Note 1].
This then is a school that has not only kept its unique vision alive, it has
also passed the tests of a school's success that had been set over its thirty
years. (Goodson & Foote, 2001)

In this case, holding educators accountable for standardized test scores
would not improve student achievement because the school's definition
of student achievement was unrelated to test scores.

Holding educators accountable has varying outcomes, just as does providing additional resources. It is inconsistent to argue that accountability
improves student achievement but additional funding does not, but this is
the reasoning behind the standards and accountability movement.

Why don't school personnel, researchers, and policymakers see this
inconsistency? One reason is that their interests are served by the assumption that teachers and principals should be held accountable for
higher student test scores.

First, teachers' and principals' interests are served because a focus on
test scores relieves them of accomplishing more complex purposes. Now
that higher student achievement is synonymous with higher test scores,
teachers and principals across the nation are taking Rhee's (2007) approach—sitting down with test score results and making plans to improve them. This is much simpler than pursuing other, more meaningful
purposes.

The standards and accountability movement also benefits researchers. They generate and explain the research findings that *theoretically*
tell teachers and principals how to improve student test scores.

This movement also serves the interests of policymakers. As Rhee
(2007) explained, the main responsibility of senior administrators and
policymakers is to hold teachers and principals accountable for student test scores. It does not matter that higher test scores are among

the shallowest of educational achievements; it only matters that test scores provide data for which teachers and principals can be held accountable.

Even though standards and accountability do not improve public education, assuming that they do serves the interests of these groups. Why else would public education be so focused on improving what is so unimportant?

MODELS THAT PRECEDED STANDARDS AND ACCOUNTABILITY

The twin pillars of standards and accountability prevent educators from addressing a wide range of student needs. What should teachers and principals do? Instead of arguing that public education should educate the whole child, they should argue for an educational foundation that allows them to balance the achievement of deeper, more meaningful purposes.

Before standards and accountability focused academic achievement discourse on higher test scores, teachers and principals achieved multiple purposes. Three sets of these purposes, and the related curricular debates and visions of the future are illustrated in figures 5.2, 5.3, and 5.4.

Public schools have traditionally been devoted to modeling and teaching three virtues (understanding, strong character, and generosity) and three vices (intellectual incompetence, fear, and pride). These are listed in the bases of figures 5.2 and 5.3.

Without the pillars of standards and accountability, educators adjusted their purposes in varying situations. This is depicted by a base that can rock back and forth to address the varying needs of students.

The middle band of figure 5.2 depicts a curriculum debate about lessons that teach about the past versus those that teach about the future. Public schools are expected to teach both, and their appropriate balance is continually debated. School personnel use judgment to balance the curriculum so students learn both our traditions and the skills needed in the future.

The top part of figure 5.2 indicates that this curriculum prepares students to be members of a democratic society. This idea goes back to

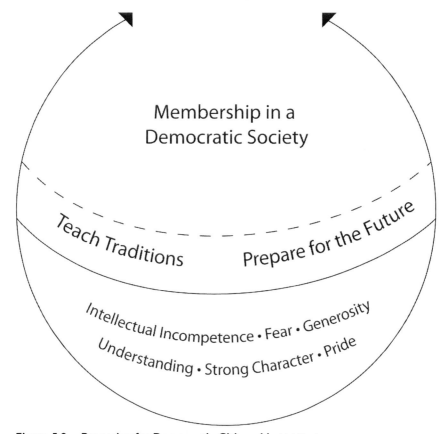

Figure 5.2. Preparing for Democratic Citizenship Neil Torda

the common school movement. It is one of the fundamental ideals of American public education.

Figure 5.3 has the same base. In this case, the curricular debate is about the proper balance of academic and vocational coursework.

When the emphasis is on academic knowledge and skills, students are being prepared for college. When the emphasis is on vocational knowledge and skills, students are being prepared for future employment. These two visions of a student's future are listed at the top.

Figure 5.4 illustrates a curriculum debate between those who argue for teaching Western civilization's core knowledge, and those who argue for teaching multicultural perspectives. This debate concerns the best

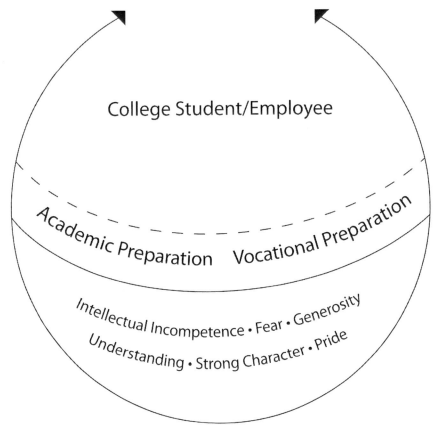

College Student/Employee

Academic Preparation   Vocational Preparation

Intellectual Incompetence • Fear • Generosity
Understanding • Strong Character • Pride

Figure 5.3.   Preparing for Work or College Neil Torda

way to prepare students for membership in a diverse society. This vision of the future is at the top.

The purposes at the base of figure 5.4 are different from earlier ones because both sides of the debate assume young people should develop pride in their heritage. Therefore, both "Pride" and "Understanding" are bold.

Our misunderstanding of pride and humility prevents us from resolving this debate between the core knowledge of Western civilization and a multicultural perspective. If we understood that humility is a virtue and pride is a vice, however, we would model and teach humility, and students would learn about both the beautiful and ugly aspects of all human traditions.

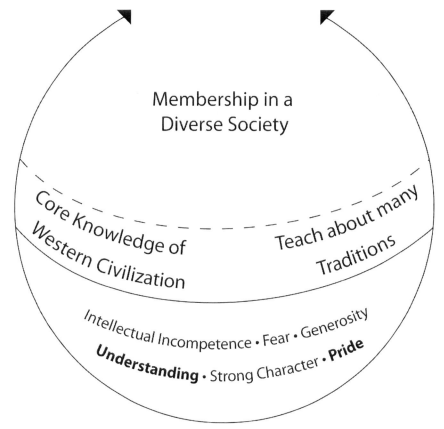

Figure 5.4. Preparing for Citizenship in a Western Society Neil Torda

THREE NEW MODELS

To complete this discussion of how purposes are related to debates about curriculum and visions of the future, three newer models are presented. The first is from Armstrong's (2006) descriptions of "Academic Achievement Discourse" and "Human Development Discourse" in *The Best Schools*. The second is from Parker's (2005) article "Teaching Against Idiocy." The third is the alternative model's proposal for its purposes, its curriculum, and its vision of the future.

Figure 5.5 illustrates Armstrong's (2006) model. He does not take issue with current public school purposes, so the base lists the same virtues and vices taught in our current model. The middle band reflects

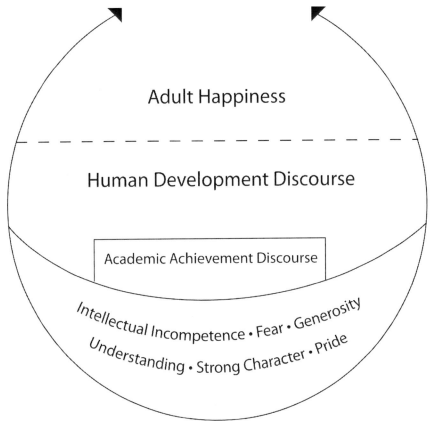

Figure 5.5. Armstrong's Model Neil Torda

his belief that curriculum should address both academic achievement and human development.

Unlike the curriculum debates in the middle bands of the earlier figures, Armstrong's curriculum does not attempt to balance competing ideas. Instead, academic achievement discourse is a subset of human development discourse. He believes education is an avenue to adult happiness, so that vision of the future is listed at the top.

Figure 5.6 illustrates Parker's (2005) belief that public schools should teach against "idiocy."

He argues that we come into the world as idiots, the meaning of which he takes from the Greek root, "idios," meaning focused on the self. He proposes that public education's purpose is to replace private vices with public virtues. This idea is expressed in the base.

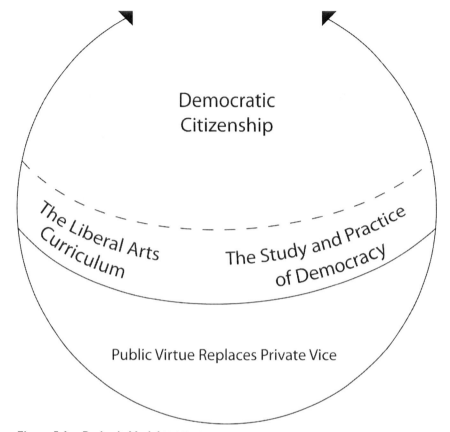

Figure 5.6. Parker's Model Neil Torda

He also argues for a liberal arts curriculum complemented by "the study and practice of democracy" (p. 351). The middle band depicts these two aspects of the curriculum. Parker (2005) believes public education should prepare students for democratic citizenship, which is the vision of the future listed at the top.

Parker's (2005) conceptualization is similar to the alternative model described in chapter 3. Both have virtue purposes, and Parker's description of "idiocy" is similar to the alternative model's description of our uneducated human nature.

The alternative model's six virtues are listed in the base of figure 5.7. They focus educators and policymakers on the purpose of modeling and teaching all six. None of them, not even understanding, is a dominant

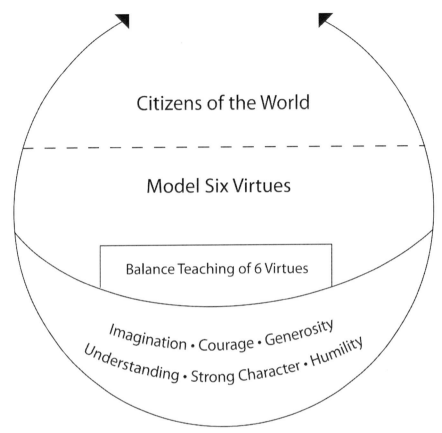

Figure 5.7.   The Alternative Model Purposes and Vision Neil Torda

purpose because the virtues cannot be separated out as they are modeled and taught in school situations.

This is completely different from saying schools ought to teach "public virtue," which is like saying we ought to teach the whole child. Neither of those ideas is specific enough to guide educators.

The middle band of figure 5.7 depicts a curriculum that models and teaches the six virtues in the tested, hidden, and extra curricula.

The top part of the circle indicates a vision of the future in which all graduates consider themselves citizens of the world. Successful graduates are those who continually develop the six virtues as the basis for living in peace with all others.

In summary, figure 5.1 illustrates that public education purposes are now held in place by the twin pillars of the standards and accountability movement. This movement focuses policymakers on holding educators accountable for students' standardized test scores. Figures 5.2 through 5.4 illustrate purposes and curriculum debates that have surfaced throughout our history. Figures 5.5 and 5.6 represent models with purposes and curricula that go beyond a focus on standardized test scores. Figure 5.7 illustrates what the alternative model looks like within this template of purposes, curricula, and vision of the future.

BARRIERS TO VIRTUE-BASED PURPOSES

Just as barriers exist to adopting a core belief that defines the educated person as one who develops the six virtues, barriers exist to adopting a virtue-based set of purposes. Even though the teaching of virtues has been a purpose of education throughout history, the standards and accountability movement has pushed public education away from virtue purposes.

The first barrier to adopting a virtue-based set of purposes is that Americans no longer describe educational purposes in terms of virtue development. For example, in Armstrong's (2006, p. 47) book about human development the only time "virtue" appears is when Roman emperor Marcus Aurelius is quoted. Similarly, in three *Educational Leadership* issues devoted to educating the whole child (September 2005, May 2007, and Online, summer 2007), the word "virtue" appears only twice.

In one case Scherer (2007) quotes Diane Ravitch's reference to civic virtue:

> Education must aim for far more than mastery of the basics, far more than the possession of tools for economic competitiveness. Certainly it should aim for enough [content] for an examined life, enough for civic virtue, and enough for those mental habits that incline one to think, to read, to listen, to discuss, to feel just a bit uncertain about one's opinions, and to love learning. (*Education Week*, January 30, 2007)

Ravitch's reference to "civic virtue" is like Parker's (2005) reference to "public virtue." Neither phrase is defined, so neither provides guidance to policymakers and school personnel.

Failing to use the word "virtue" is not a criticism of the *Educational Leadership* contributors. Many of them are outstanding thinkers, like Noddings, Eisner, Armstrong, Rothstein, Wilder, Jacobsen, Castleman, and Littky (to name a few). The point is that both the word and the concept of "virtue" are absent from discussions of American public school purposes. Why is that?

The main reason was mentioned earlier—that public educators associate virtues with religion. Ever since school-sponsored prayer was ruled unconstitutional in 1962, public school educators distance themselves from teaching anything that can be construed as religious. Ravitch's phrase "civic virtue" and Parker's phrase "public virtue" are examples of how public educators' discussions of virtue need to be stripped of religious associations.

The Clinton administration distributed a statement on "Religious Expression in Public Schools" that clarified acceptable and unacceptable public school engagements with religion. I don't know of any policy-makers and educators who read this report and thought, "Great! Now we can teach secular virtues, even if they could be construed as having religious connections." Instead, when it comes to religion in schools, a fear of First Amendment lawsuits is powerful.

A second barrier to virtue purposes is that public education has been moving in the opposite direction for the past 20 years. A virtue-based set of purposes requires a complete reversal of what Americans have been demanding from public education. Instead of a narrow, easily measured set of purposes, they have to demand a broad set of purposes that are difficult to measure. Instead of an exclusive focus on test scores, they have to demand that school personnel model and teach six virtues that cannot be measured by numbers.

A third barrier is the belief that the main purpose of public education is to teach academic knowledge and skills. For many, this means public schools should leave other areas of human development to families and churches. This may be a strong sentiment among teachers and parents, but it reflects a kind of fragmentary thinking that contradicts human experience. The education of young people is never just about academic knowledge and skills.

OVERCOMING THE BARRIERS

All three of these barriers can be overcome. The first is the terminology problem. Some may ask, if the word "virtue" frightens public school educators because of religious associations, why doesn't the alternative model describe the educated person as one who develops six "traits," six "qualities," or six "dispositions?" Why insist on "six virtues?"

One reason is that teaching virtue has a rich philosophical tradition. The teaching of virtue is discussed by Aristotle, Thomas Aquinas, Kant, and many others. Recently, MacIntyre (1999) has argued that we need a return to teaching virtue.

The concept of virtue connects public education with this rich tradition. Why leave the teaching of virtue to parochial schools? We already speak of "civic virtues" and "public virtues." The alternative model is proposing that understanding, imagination, strong character, courage, humility, and generosity can be the specific "civic" or "public" virtues that public schools teach.

Another reason to use "virtue" is that it has an opposite in the word "vice." These opposing terms enable us to discuss the vices we overcome as we become educated. We are born in a state of ignorance, intellectual incompetence, weakness, fear, pride, and selfishness. Educated adults are those who overcome these vices as they develop understanding, imagination, strength, courage, humility, and generosity. "Traits," "qualities," or "dispositions" do not have opposites that capture this distinction between our uneducated and educated human natures.

A third reason to use the word "virtue" is that virtues are both ways of being and ways of acting. "Traits," "qualities," or "dispositions" describe either capacities or abilities—but not both. The world does not get better if people with understanding do not act with imagination, if those with strong character do not act with courage, or if humble people are not also generous. What good is an educated citizenry if it does not make the world better? Only citizens who develop both virtuous capacities and virtuous abilities can make the world better.

To overcome the barrier of going in the opposite direction, public educators can take comfort in knowing that the standards and accountability movement's focus on standardized test scores is a recent development. During most of the 20th century, public educators pursued and balanced more meaningful purposes.

And reversing direction has many supporters. ASCD promotes teaching the whole child; and Armstrong (2006) argues eloquently for a human development curriculum. The time is right for like-minded persons and public educators to establish this deep, meaningful set of virtue purposes for public education.

Finally, instead of believing public schools should only teach academic knowledge and skills, we can reject fragmentary thinking of this kind because it conflicts with human experience. Elkind and Sweet (2007b) make this point as they address public educators:

> Let's get one thing perfectly clear—you are a character educator. Whether you are a teacher, administrator, custodian, or school bus driver, you are helping to shape the character of the kids you come in contact with. It's in the way you talk, the behaviors you model, the conduct you tolerate, the deeds you encourage, the expectations you transmit. Yes, for better or for worse, you already are doing character education.

This chapter started with the same point. Whether or not public education "should" have purposes other than the teaching of academic skills is a moot point. Young people are never educated in ways that are only academic.

CONCLUSION

The standards and accountability movement has narrowed the purpose of public education to teaching the understanding that improves standardized test scores. The alternative model purposes are stated in terms of the virtues that define what it means to be educated. The next chapter describes the importance of modeling these virtues in the way public education is governed.

6

EDUCATIONAL GOVERNANCE

Figure 1.1 illustrates our current model of public education. Governance is the second element and purpose is the third because elected officials establish the purposes of public education.

Americans assume the purposes of American public education should emerge from a democratic process. They also assume that those who want to shape educational purposes, including teachers and principals, should do so by engaging in the politics of education. Both assumptions are challenged in this chapter.

The first is challenged by arguing that purpose should be the second element of our model of education and governance should be the third. This change enables public education to be governed in accordance with what it means to be educated, instead of in accordance with the interests of elected officials.

The second assumption is challenged by arguing that teachers and principals should not participate in the democratic governance of public education. Those who participate disqualify themselves from arguing that educational governance should replace political governance. At this point in history, it is more important to establish the former than to improve the latter.

WHY NOT DEMOCRATIC GOVERNANCE?

Education should not be governed democratically for the simple reason that students learn what is modeled by adults. When policymakers and school personnel model virtue, students learn virtue. When they model vice, students learn vice. Unfortunately, democratic governance models and promotes more vice than virtue.

This section discusses the practice of democratic politics by asking two questions:

- Do elected officials demonstrate humility and promote understanding, imagination, strong character, courage, and generosity?
- Or do they demonstrate pride and promote ignorance, intellectual incompetence, weakness, fear, and selfishness?

Humility is necessary for the development of the other five virtues, so its role is discussed first. Do candidates for school board and state legislative offices model humility or pride?

Humble candidates for public office do not win elections, but proud ones do. Candidates who display humility shine a light on the accomplishments of others; proud ones shine a light on themselves and cast a shadow on opponents. As this happens, proud candidates are elected to school boards and state legislatures. The election of proud candidates, instead of humble ones, suggests that our high school graduates don't know the difference between virtue and vice. This tells us more about what students learn than do student test scores, which are a proxy for understanding and tell us nothing about the other five virtues.

Do the proud candidates elected to office promote understanding and imagination, or ignorance and intellectual incompetence? Remember—proud people seek the light and cast a shadow on others. Political campaigns are dominated by 30-second television and radio ads that promote voter incompetence. They insult voter intelligence, but political research has found that they win elections. This also tells us more about what students learn in public schools than do their test scores. Our imaginations are so dull that we consistently elect candidates who fill the most advertising space with platitudes.

Do politicians promote strong character and courage, or weakness and fear? In the 1964 presidential campaign, Johnson attacked Goldwater with a nuclear bomb image that appealed to voter fear. And in the 1988 presidential campaign, Bush attacked former Massachusetts governor Michael Dukakis with the image of Willie Horton, a convicted felon who kidnapped, stabbed, and raped while on a weekend furlough from a Massachusetts prison. Both Johnson and Bush were elected in landslides. This also tells us more about what students learn in public schools than do their test scores. Americans vote for candidates who appeal to fears, instead of for those who have the courage to admit they cannot keep us safe.

Finally, do politicians promote generosity or selfishness? Incumbents have the advantage of reminding constituents of the "pork" they acquire for their home districts. West Virginia Senator Robert Byrd is renowned for bringing pork-barrel spending to West Virginia. Instead of being ashamed of abusing his power, he has used it to get reelected eight times. State and federal incumbents are rarely defeated for reelection. Not only do candidates appeal to voter selfishness, but bringing home the "pork" is the greatest political virtue—another way in which American democratic politics confuses vice for virtue, and another way in which this confusion tells us more about what students learn in public schools than do their test scores.

Americans consistently elect educational governors who model pride and promote ignorance, intellectual incompetence, fear, and selfishness. Until these elected officials and their appointees model virtue, public school graduates will continue to be uneducated in ways that are more profound than their inability to correctly answer multiple-choice questions.

The first point of this chapter is that political governance is antieducational because those who win political office model and promote our uneducated human nature. Elected officials achieve their purposes through the exercise of power, but they must get reelected to use it. Therefore, even those who are imaginative, courageous, and humble demonstrate a lack of imagination (stay on message), model pride (claim they are proud of their country), and promote fear (paint their opponent as a risk) in order to get re-elected. If they are good enough at modeling and promoting these vices, they get re-elected, gain power, and make the world worse—all at the same time.

The purpose of education, however, is to make the world better. This happens whenever adults model and promote the six virtues, but this is rare in politics. Democratically elected officials who feel a need to get reelected model what it means to be a political person instead of an educated one. This dysfunction is avoided in a model in which purpose precedes governance. And this is one way that the alternative model is fundamentally different from our current model.

CAN DEMOCRATIC GOVERNANCE IMPROVE PUBLIC EDUCATION?

Some of the guest speakers in my graduate classes have been dedicated, well-intentioned North Carolina state legislators. As they describe various legislative initiatives, it is clear that they have all kinds of ideas about how to improve public schools.

It is equally clear, though, that none of their ideas are based on a deep, meaningful definition of what it means to be educated. In the absence of such a definition, they promote educational purposes like preparing students to compete in a global economy, getting back to basics, or improving SAT scores.

An extremely small part of being educated is the ability to join a global workforce, to do basic math algorithms, or to answer SAT questions. The priority given to these purposes illustrates that American public education is driven by the economic and political interests of those who govern. But this is not a conspiracy. It is simply what happens when elected officials establish educational purposes, or when governance precedes purpose.

We are in a Catch-22 situation. We want better schools, but we elect officials who cannot make them better because, in order to get elected, they must model pride and promote fear, selfishness, and intellectual incompetence—vices of our uneducated nature.

These are damning accusations. Where is the evidence for concluding that democratically elected officials cannot improve public education?

One set of evidence emerges from an analysis of Brubaker and Nelson's (1974) *Creative Survival in Educational Bureaucracies*. In this book, the authors assume public education must be governed politically. Their main contribution to the education literature is the recommendation that political governance works best when the bureaucratic and professional aspects of public education are "married" to one another.

We have more than 30 years of trying what Brubaker and Nelson (1974) recommended, so we have historical evidence of the results we get after trying to make this "marriage" work. We can examine this evidence by asking three questions:

- What did the authors recommend in 1974?
- What has happened since then?
- What can we learn from this history?

Looking back through history, we can see if the "marriage" worked, and we can ask why things turned out the way they did.

Brubaker and Nelson (1974) wrote what readers of this book are probably thinking right now—education is a government function, so it must be governed politically:

> We can best understand the school and its operations if we view the school as a governmental operation. The schools are designed to implement the objectives of the state, local, and federal governments, and as such are an expression of these governments. (p. 60)

My graduate students say the same thing all the time. I am not sure why public education has to be governed politically, but many people believe this to be true.

Brubaker and Nelson (1974, p. x) recommended "a marriage between the bureaucratic and professional models in educational organizations." According to them, a bureaucratic structure is needed to provide compliance with rules and clear lines of authority, and a professional structure is needed because the instructional program should be governed by the "expert judgments of professionals rather than the disciplined compliance with the commands of superiors" (p. 67).

In other words, public education should be organized as a bureaucracy (because it is a government function), and the bureaucracy should be "married" to a professional structure in which teachers and principals use professional judgment to carry out instructional purposes.

A "marriage" between bureaucratic and professional structures makes sense. Citizens and educators alike believe public schools should be governed by school boards, state legislatures, and federal departments of education; they also believe instructional judgments should be made by school professionals working closely with students. Brubaker and Nelson's (1974) marriage metaphor captures the way we have tried to govern public education for the latter part of the 20th century and the beginning of the 21st century. With more than 30 years of this marriage behind us, how has it worked?

Since *A Nation at Risk*, the bureaucratic partner has usurped the prerogatives of the professional one. States have taken control of education, resulting in centralized control of curriculum, and centralized control of the assessment of students and teachers. What had been controlled at the local level is now politicized and controlled by state and federal legislatures. What may have been a good idea in 1974 has become a marriage that does not work because the bureaucratic partner oppresses and disrespects the professional one.

For example, since the passage of NCLB, each state's achievement testing program must be approved by federal officials. State departments of public instruction try to convince federal officials that "at grade level" should be set at a low threshold, so more of its schools achieve adequate yearly progress. Federal officials reject thresholds that are too low so the Department of Education can appear to hold educators accountable for achieving high standards instead of low ones. This arrangement results in a political definition of "at grade level" that disregards professional educators' knowledge of individual students' abilities and situations.

Governing public education through a marriage of bureaucratic and professional approaches made sense in 1974 and we are still trying to make it work. The result is a failed marriage in which the professional partner has no recourse. When teachers and principals argue against political and bureaucratic initiatives, they are considered self-interested obstructionists.

With hindsight we can see that this marriage was doomed from the beginning. Failing to reverse governance and purpose, Brubaker and Nelson (1974) proposed a marriage in which the professional partner would be silenced as governance moved to the state and federal levels.

It is time to file for divorce and use this recent oppression of teachers and principals to argue for a model in which educational purposes precede governance. This brings us to the second assumption challenged in this chapter.

SHOULD EDUCATORS PARTICIPATE IN THE POLITICS OF EDUCATION?

My colleagues and graduate students are puzzled when I say teachers and principals should not participate in educational politics because they have been taught to believe they should be active in the democratic politics of public education. I take the opposite position for three reasons.

First, participating in educational politics gives legitimacy to the belief that public education should be governed politically. For example, when teachers and principals lobby for fuller funding of NCLB, they are affirming a federal role in public education.

Second, participating in educational politics prevents teachers and principals from arguing for educational governance. If they don't explain why public education should be governed educationally, nobody will. They are the only ones whose school experiences enable them to see the antieducational nature of democratic politics. Only they know that public education does not achieve the educational purposes for which it was established whenever the political interests of adults are more important than the interests of students.

The third reason is that nothing is lost if teachers and principals stay out of educational politics. Their involvement has not improved public education so far, and it is unlikely to do so in the future.

Telling educators not to participate in educational politics contradicts all who say they should. Why do so many say this?

A review of Richard Elmore and Susan Fuhrman's recommendations in the 1994 ASCD yearbook, *The Governance of Curriculum*, addresses this question. Similar to the way Brubaker and Nelson's (1974) ideas were studied, Elmore and Fuhrman's (1994a, 1994b) recommendations can be examined by asking the same three questions: What did they recommend in 1994? What has happened since then? What can we learn from this history?

Elmore and Fuhrman's (1994a) recommendation that teachers and principals should engage in the politics of education framed the purpose of their book:

> This yearbook attempts to lay out the terms of the present national debate on educational reform, educational standards, and governance in a way that is relevant to educational professionals whose primary responsibility lies within schools and districts. We believe that the consequences of this broader debate depend heavily on whether and how education professionals choose to play a part. In a sense this book is a short course in the politics of curriculum reform and governance, designed to provide the wherewithal for educational professionals to play a more prominent and effective role in the current policy debates. (p. 2)

Their belief that "the consequences of this broader debate depend heavily on whether and how education professionals choose to play a part" is the point challenged in this chapter.

It is being challenged because, when governance precedes purpose, educational policymaking begins with politics, ends with politics, and depends on politics throughout. The efforts of educators are of little or no consequence.

The following is a study of the recommendations Elmore and Fuhrman (1994b) offered in the final chapter. Their first recommendation (Elmore & Fuhrman, 1994b) was that educators should develop expertise:

> Most policymakers recognize their limitations and look to people with expertise for advice. But expertise is often a fragile and perishable commodity in policy debates. Policymakers are most interested in hearing from professionals who are willing to confront the problems they, policymakers, think are important, not just the problems that professionals think are important . . . policymakers want effective expertise that focuses on the relevant problems—our second piece of advice. (pp. 213–214)

This is a clear expression of how political governance works within our current model. "Relevant problems" are those related to the agendas of policymakers; irrelevant ones are those of school professionals.

Their second recommendation is that educators should understand and accept the centralization of educational governance. Assuming an arrangement like the marriage proposed by Brubaker and Nelson (1974), they wrote: "Important daily decisions will continue to be made at the school and district level, but the context for these decisions will increasingly be shaped by strong forces from the state and national levels" (p. 214).

The third recommendation is that "Education professionals should cultivate and use professional networks to increase expertise and to exercise influence" (p. 214):

> In most instances, policymakers are sufficiently aware of their limitations in areas like curriculum policy that they will readily seek professional advice when it is well formed and articulated. Policymakers will seldom refrain from making policy, however, in the absence of sound professional advice, when they are responding to strong pressures to act.

Their reasoning recognizes that policymaking is driven by political concerns more than educational ones.

Their fourth recommendation is captured in the heading "Promote 'Best Practice,' Not Professional Self-interest" (p. 214). They assume there is a difference between "best practices" and educators' self-interest. They also assume teachers and principals can recognize the difference and choose against self-interest.

To summarize, Elmore and Fuhrman's (1994b) second and fourth recommendations tell practitioners to put self-interest aside, but their third recommendation does not ask policymakers to do the same. This book's enduring contribution may be its description of how governance actually works within our current model.

What does recent history tell us about these recommendations? Does it suggest that "the consequences of this broader debate depend heavily on whether and how education professionals choose to play a part" (p. 2)?

We cannot know the extent to which educators achieved these recommendations but, for the sake of argument, let's assume they did not accomplish them. Given that failure, which argument is more plausible—that accomplishing them would have altered our current situation, or that accomplishing them would have had little effect on our current situation?

The first argument is difficult to make. It would have to be shown that, with enough expertise, networking, and pushing against policy limits, professional educators working together since 1994 could have prevented educational governance from moving to the state level, and eventually to the federal level.

Given the extent to which states excluded local educators from efforts to legislate educational improvement during the 1990s and the ease with which NCLB hijacked those efforts in 2001, it is hard to believe that even the most politically astute and active teachers and principals could have stopped these developments.

Furthermore, Elmore and Fuhrman's (1994b) second and fourth recommendations are that professional concerns should be subordinated to those of policymakers. The rationale for this recommendation is that professional educators are self-interested. This was the same reasoning that usurped professional autonomy as governance became more centralized. Instead of preventing centralization, two of Elmore and Fuhrman's (1994b) recommendations push policymaking in that direction.

Based on 15 years of recent history, the only plausible conclusion is that achieving Elmore and Fuhrman's (1994b) recommendations would have had little effect on our current situation. Like Brubaker and Nelson (1974) before them, they assumed professional educators could influence educational governance, but they, too, were wrong.

When governance precedes purpose, teachers and principals are required to pursue the purposes established by elected officials. If becoming involved in this process makes them feel better, that is fine. But their involvement does not change the fact that, within our current model, the governance of public education serves political purposes more than educational ones. Elmore and Fuhrman (1994a, 1994b) provide a clear description of this very idea.

Political governance makes it seem normal for schools to pursue political purposes. One way to change this is to adopt a model in which purpose precedes governance. But purpose cannot precede governance until that purpose is clearly stated in a definition of what it means to be educated.

Professional educators are the only ones in a position to propose such a definition. Citizens and policymakers don't think about what it means to be educated, but teachers and principals think about it all the time. When they add imagination, courage, and humility to what they already model and teach, they will contribute more to the improvement of public education than they will by participating in democratic governance.

A LETTER TO LOCAL AND STATE POLICYMAKERS

This chapter concludes with a letter to local and state policymakers from teachers and principals who want to adopt the alternative model.

Dear Local and State Policymakers:

You have good intentions as you work to improve the education of children. Because we work with these children and are subject to your policies, we see both the good and bad that are accomplished by them.

We are sure you want us to inform you of whether we are going in the right direction or the wrong direction. That is one purpose of this letter—to tell you we are going in the wrong direction. The second purpose is to explain three suggestions for changing course and going in the right direction.

Our first suggestion is that you should ignore No Child Left Behind. The second is that you should read *Cheating Our Kids: How Politics and Greed Ruin Education* by Joe Williams, published in 2005. And the third is that you should analyze your beliefs about education and governance to see if they promote the development of virtue among students.

Accomplishing the first suggestion is an effortless way to improve public education. Federal officials are not elected to govern public education. You are. Ignoring NCLB enables you to devote time and effort to governing in a way that benefits the children in your state and district.

In the past, when you failed to provide equal educational opportunities for African American students, special needs students, and females, federal courts and legislation intervened to benefit all students, not just the disadvantaged. For example, Title IX legislation paved the way for your daughters and granddaughters to have the same opportunities your sons and grandsons always had. All of society is better for it. The same is true for federal interventions that require disabled students to be educated in the least restrictive environment, and for the outlawing of *de jure* racial segregation. Federal interventions addressing local- and state-sponsored inequalities benefit all students, but that is not true for NCLB.

Do students benefit from being tested under requirements approved by the Department of Education, instead of those you establish? Do they learn more when taught by teachers arbitrarily defined as highly qualified? Do they learn more from reading programs sponsored by friends of the president's family? (See Elaine Garan's *Resisting Reading Mandates: How to Triumph with the Truth*, published in 2002, for more information on this.)

Experience and reason tell you that federal policy achieves some goals at the expense of others. Experience and reason also tell you that you are in the best position to decide priorities, and federal officials are in the worst position.

Accommodating NCLB distracts you from governing in ways that are more likely to benefit your students. As long as you provide equal educational opportunity, which is your primary responsibility, federal officials have no reason to become involved in your state or district—especially when their requirements cause you to spend more resources on questionable practices, like teaching to the test or changing teacher assignments to accommodate an arbitrary definition of highly qualified teachers.

You don't have to tell anybody you are ignoring NCLB. Just do it.

Our second suggestion is to read *Cheating Our Kids: How Politics and Greed Ruin Education* by Joe Williams. The author is a journalist who describes urban school districts governed by corrupt politicians, incompetent administrators, self-serving teacher unions, and greedy vendors. His main point, though, applies to rural and suburban districts too. It is that adults are the beneficiaries of a politically governed system of public education.

Williams' descriptions of greed, abuse of power, incompetence, and political self-interest illustrate the antieducational underpinnings of how we govern public education. He tells these stories to argue that parent power is needed to balance the powers exercised by school board members, legislators, educational administrators, and teacher unions. He says:

> It is apparent that politics drives much of what happens in public education, which means the first step toward solving the educational problem is solving the political problem. Parents need to step forward and declare that enough is enough if their kids are not the top priority in their school systems. . . . I'm convinced that major change is possible if a critical mass of individuals comes to understand that power has been in the wrong hands for too long. Parents just may be the one group left who can save public education in America. (p. 236)

Williams believes in the democratic governance of public education, so his argument is that more parental involvement is needed to improve schools.

We want to improve public education too—but we believe the best way to do so is to adopt a model of education that puts purpose before governance. That is why we are recommending the adoption of the alternative model as described in *The Six Virtues of an Educated Person* by J. Casey Hurley, published in 2009.

After reading Williams' book, ask yourself if democratic governance can be improved with an infusion of parent power, or if the alternative model's definition of the educated person described in Hurley's book should guide the governance of public education. If you believe the first, your job is to get parents more involved in the governance of public education. If you believe the second, your job is simply to model the six virtues of the educated person in the way you govern. You control the second, but not the first, so we recommend that you join the alternative model movement described in *The Six Virtues of an Educated Person*.

This brings us to our third suggestion. You should examine the relationships among your educational and governing beliefs. The following Venn diagrams illustrate what we mean. The first diagram depicts an

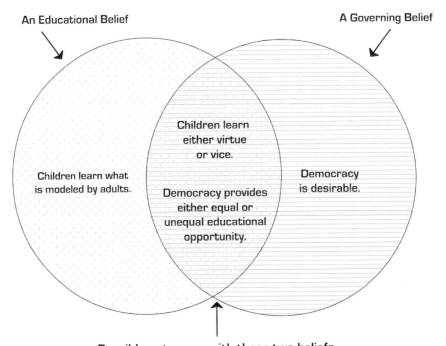

An Educational Belief

A Governing Belief

Children learn what
is modeled by adults.

Children learn
either virtue
or vice.

Democracy provides
either equal or
unequal educational
opportunity.

Democracy
is desirable.

Possible outcomes with these two beliefs

Figure 6.1. **The Intersection of Educational and Governing Beliefs** Neil Torda

example of how these beliefs overlap each other and the results that are possible within them.

The left sphere holds one of your beliefs about public education. It is that "Children learn what is modeled by adults." That is the belief that causes you to fire a teacher who models inappropriate behavior.

The right sphere represents your beliefs about governance. One belief is that "Democracy is a desirable form of governance."

The intersection of these two sets of beliefs can yield different outcomes. Two possible outcomes are listed where the spheres overlap. One outcome is that, depending on the behavior you model, students will learn to be either virtuous or vicious. The second is that, depending on how you fund public education, students will experience whether or not democratic governance is as desirable for children living in poor districts as it is for those living in wealthy ones.

Figure 6.2 illustrates these same beliefs with the two most likely outcomes within our current model. Because governance precedes

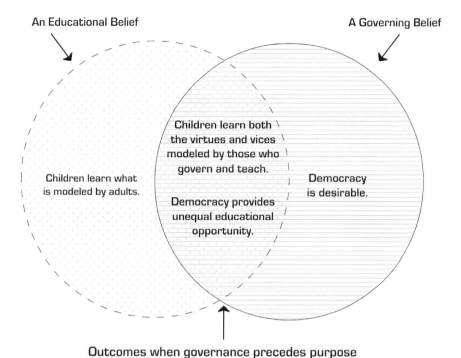

An Educational Belief

A Governing Belief

Children learn both
the virtues and vices
modeled by those who
govern and teach.

Children learn what
is modeled by adults.

Democracy
is desirable.

Democracy provides
unequal educational
opportunity.

Outcomes when governance precedes purpose

Figure 6.2.   Governing Beliefs Are Primary Neil Torda

purpose, governing beliefs take priority over educational ones. That is why the sphere of governing beliefs is a solid line, and the sphere of educational beliefs is a dashed line.

Public schools teach understanding that is unimaginative, strong character that is fearful, and generosity that emerges from pride. That is why the first outcome listed in figure 6.3 is that "Children learn both the virtues and vices modeled by those who govern and teach."

The second outcome is that "Democratic governance provides unequal educational opportunity" because few states provide anything close to equal educational opportunity for children in property-poor districts.

On the other hand, if you adopt the alternative model for schools, your educational beliefs would take precedence over governance beliefs, and you would get the results listed in figure 6.3.

The education beliefs sphere is a solid line and the governing beliefs sphere is a dashed one because education precedes governance. In this model, your educational responsibility is to model understanding,

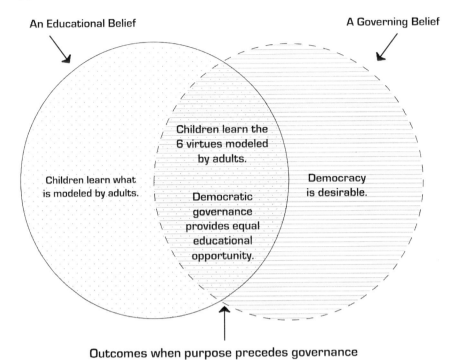

Figure 6.3. Educational Beliefs Are Primary Neil Torda

imagination, strength, courage, humility, and generosity; and your governance responsibility is to provide equal educational opportunity. Both outcomes are listed where the two belief systems overlap.

If equal educational opportunity is to be more than an empty phrase, you are the ones who must provide it. This is your primary responsibility. Your *imagination* must find ways to provide poor children with opportunities equal to those of middle- and upper-class children. You must have the *courage* to propose and support legislation that equalizes funding. And your *generosity* must emerge from a humble belief in the beauty and worth of all children.

Thanks for considering these three suggestions. The best way to accomplish all three is to adopt the alternative model described in chapter 3 of *The Six Virtues of an Educated Person.*

Sincerely,
Teachers and principals

7

CHILDREN LEARN IN COMMUNITY

So far, the alternative model's core belief, purposes, and governance have all been different from those of our current model. Organizational structure is the fourth element. In this case, it appears as though both models agree that schools should be organized as communities.

Teachers have a saying that recognizes the power of community: "Students don't care how much you know, until they know how much you care." Similarly, school reformers believe community is a key to school improvement.

The Bill and Melinda Gates Foundation sponsors "schools within schools" in the belief that students learn better in small, communal environments. And the school reform literature promotes the idea of professional learning communities (PLCs). According to Schmoker (2004, p. 424): "Milbrey McLaughlin speaks for a legion of esteemed educators and researchers when she asserts that 'the *most promising strategy* for sustained, substantive school improvement is building the capacity of school personnel to function as a professional learning community'" (emphasis added by Schmoker).

Four years later, Hargreaves (2008) wrote:

Professional learning communities (PLCs) are no longer unusual or controversial. Their advent is over, their establishment secured. While researchers and developers push them ahead by showing how they can become more effective and mature (McLaughlin & Talbert, 2006), professional learning communities will soon be as accepted a part of school life as notebooks, performance evaluations, and good old fashioned chalk. (p. 175)

Professional learning communities are universally promoted in the school reform literature. Are these the communitarian structures required in the alternative model?

Unfortunately, they are not. According to the language describing PLCs, they are structures that promote a sense of community, but they are not actual communities. Bryk, Lee, and Holland (1993, p. 275) made this distinction in their analysis of Catholic high schools. According to them, "In the Catholic schools we visited, members said 'We *are* a community,' not 'We have a *sense* of community'" (italics in original).

The fourth element of the alternative model requires schools to be communities. It is not enough for them to be bureaucratic structures with a sense of community, which is how PLCs are described throughout the literature.

Since 1978, I have been involved with public education as a high school administrator, professor of educational administration, and parent of public school children. All my prior educational experiences were in Catholic schools. The most fundamental difference between these two types of institutions is that public schools are bureaucratic and Catholic schools are communitarian.

Ever since PLCs have been regarded as "the *most promising strategy* for sustained, substantive school improvement" (Schmoker, 2004), I have wondered if they are like the Catholic school communities I experienced. The answer can be found by comparing the language used to describe PLCs with the language used by Bryk, Lee, and Holland (1993) to describe seven carefully selected Catholic high schools.

PLCS REFLECT BUREAUCRATIC BELIEFS

Americans believe public education should be organized in a bureaucratic hierarchy so educators can be held accountable for student learning. The following four questions emerge from this belief:

- Who should be held accountable?
- Who should hold them accountable?
- For what should they be held accountable?
- How should schools be structured for this function?

The PLC literature addresses all four questions.

Hord and Hirsh (2008, p. 24) point to the first word in the phrase "professional learning communities" to explain that the members of PLCs are the school professionals. PLCs are consistently described as collaborative teams of teachers and administrators (Dufour, Eaker, & Dufour, 2005; Hord & Hirsh, 2008; Schmoker, 2005; Stoll, Bolam, Mc-Mahon, Wallace, & Thomas, 2006).

A strictly professional PLC membership reflects the belief that professional educators should be held accountable for student learning. This raises the question of who should hold them accountable.

Teachers and principals are supposed to be held accountable by locally elected officials and their appointees. The standards and accountability movement recently extended this responsibility to state and federal officials. Elected officials at all three levels now hire senior administrators to hold school personnel accountable.

According to PLC proponents, the school-improvement literature provides evidence that student achievement improves when schools form PLCs. This raises the third question: What is meant by student achievement; or, for what should school professionals be held accountable?

Although PLC proponents claim to define student learning more broadly than test scores, their descriptions of PLCs reflect an obsession with test-score data. For example, to illustrate what they mean by a "results orientation," Dufour and Eaker (1998) presented a fictional account of a first-year teacher's experience within a PLC. Connie (the

fictional teacher) went through an orientation that included an afternoon session in which:

> the team analyzed student performance according to the common assess-
> ment instruments from the previous year, identified areas where students
> did not meet the desired proficiencies established by the team, and
> discussed strategies for improving student performance. The discussion
> helped Connie understand what students were to accomplish, how they
> were to be assessed, and where they had experienced difficulties in the
> past. She found the discussion to be invaluable. (p. 34)

Evidently, a "results orientation" is a focus on test scores. It would require more than an afternoon session to understand results related to
how well students were prepared for college, work, or participation in a
democratic society.

To be fair, it should be pointed out that the last paragraph of Dufour
and Eaker's (1998) fictional account explicitly states that PLC members
go beyond trying to improve test scores:

> Every teacher was called on to ask him- or herself each day, "How can I
> be more effective in my efforts to be a positive influence in the lives of
> the students entrusted to me?" Yet it was equally clear that teachers were
> never to conclude that they had arrived at *the* definitive answer to any
> fundamental question. (p. 44)

Which is it? Does a "results orientation" mean teachers rely on test-
score answers to questions about "what students were to accomplish,
how they were to be assessed, and where they had experienced dif-
ficulties in the past" (p. 34)? Or are teachers "never to conclude that
they had arrived at *the* definitive answer to any fundamental question"
(p. 44)?

As a Catholic high school teacher, I took the second position; but
PLC proponents, like Schmoker (2006), consistently argue the first:

> We have to be clear about what true teamwork entails: a regular schedule
> of formal meetings where teachers focus on the details of their lessons
> and adjust them on the basis of assessment results. The use of common
> assessments is essential here. Without these, teams can't discern or enjoy
> the impact of their efforts on an ongoing basis. (p. 108)

Clearly, those who insist on a "results orientation" are insisting on a test-score focus.

PLCs are focused on test-score results because policymakers have steered public education toward that purpose. The primary reason PLCs are universally promoted in the school improvement literature is that they have been shown to improve test scores.

The fourth question asks how schools should be structured for this accountability purpose. According to Gifford and Elizabeth Pinchot (1993, p. 50), "When we think of organizing, the idea of hierarchy leaps to mind, or a picture of an 'organization chart' in the shape of a pyramid." But it is more than thinking in terms of an organizational pyramid that makes bureaucratic hierarchy the default for public education.

As explained in chapter 1, in our current model, the elements on the left influence those to the right. A bureaucratic organizational structure emerges from the belief that school personnel must be held accountable for achieving the purposes identified by elected officials.

Both Fullan (2005) and Hargreaves (2008) described how PLCs are related to the bureaucratic context that surrounds them. Fullan (2005) warned that PLCs are vulnerable to the community-destroying forces of the larger bureaucratic context:

> I will argue that if we do not examine and improve the overall system at three levels, we will never have more than temporary havens of excellence that come and go. Without attention to the larger system, professional learning communities will always be in the minority, never rising above 20% in popularity in the nation, and will not last beyond the tenure of those fortunate to have established temporary collaborative cultures. (p. 210)

Fullan (2005) wants to replace the political, bureaucratic structures that surround PLCs with community-tolerant ones. His concern about the vulnerability of PLCs within bureaucracies is illustrated in figure 7.1.

The circle represents PLCs and their features of teamwork, collaboration, collective planning, and action. The smallest triangle represents the public school bureaucracy. The three larger triangular structures represent the bureaucracies of the school district, the state department of public instruction, and the federal Department of Education.

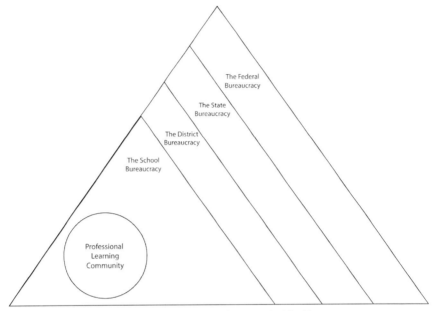

Figure 7.1. PLCs Are Vulnerable to and Surrounded by Bureaucracy Neil Torda

I agree that PLCs are vulnerable, but I don't share Fullan's (2005) concern because I consider them to be bureaucratic structures that promote a *sense* of community rather than true communities. If they were true communities, they would pursue deep, meaningful purposes identified by those who work with children, not shallow ones identified by those outside the school community.

Hargreaves' (2008) position is like mine. He distinguished between PLCs that are communities of containment and control, and those that are communities of empowerment. According to him, in communities of the first type, teacher professionalism is undermined and student test scores are sometimes improved at the expense of learning. On the other hand, he described the second type of PLCs as communities that "heighten the capacity for community reflection that is at the heart of teacher professionalism" (p. 176). He explained that these empowered communities are living, learning, inclusive, responsive, and activist.

These are the same qualities that describe both my own Catholic high school experiences and the cultures of the Catholic high schools studied by Bryk, Lee, and Holland (1993). And these are the same qualities that distinguish *actual* communities from bureaucratic structures that promote a *sense* of community.

In summary, the PLCs described in the school improvement literature are not actual communities for several reasons. They are structures in which professional educators collaborate to achieve purposes defined by those outside the PLC. They may promote a sense of community, but they are part of the public school bureaucracy that serves political and bureaucratic purposes more than educational and communitarian ones.

HIGH SCHOOLS THAT ARE COMMUNITIES

If PLCs are not the communities required in the alternative model, what are? Examples can be found among parochial schools. To describe the communities required in the alternative model, I draw from my own Catholic school experiences and Bryk, Lee, and Holland's (1993) descriptions of seven carefully selected Catholic high schools.

The following beliefs drive the educational experiences of students in these school communities:

- All community members, including students and parents, are responsible for student learning.
- Community membership involves shared values.
- Student achievement is human development in intellectual, character, and spiritual domains.
- Students develop in these domains if they are schooled within a community.

These beliefs contrast sharply with the beliefs of PLC proponents, and they give meaning to the distinction between an *actual* community and a bureaucratic structure that promotes a *sense* of community.

I attended a K–8 Catholic school and graduated from a Catholic high school in 1970. In the fall of 1974, I returned to my high school to teach and coach. In 1977, I left to pursue a master's degree in educational administration.

My first public school experience was as a full-time, intern assistant principal in 1978. The first thing that struck me in this role was that students had no responsibility to the school community. The official attitude among public school adults was that their purpose was to serve students, and this needed to be done without requiring anything in return.

Of course schools serve students, but a hole is created in the education of young people when they have no responsibility for contributing anything in return. Public school students learn from school board members, administrators, teachers, and parents that they are clients of a bureaucracy, not members of a community.

In contrast, my Catholic school experiences taught me that everyone was responsible for contributing to the community. I learned this as a student and I taught it as a teacher and coach. So did my colleagues and other community members.

In my role as a public high school assistant principal, however, I learned not to ask students to contribute to the school. When I counseled truant or disruptive students, they laughed at me for suggesting that their behavior reflected poorly on the school, or that they had a responsibility to make the school better. I still hear their laughter and see their disbelief.

Like others around them, they considered themselves clients to be served by bureaucratic functionaries. Nobody regarded them as members of a community for which they shared a responsibility. The significance of this distinction is of great importance to a young person's education.

Those public school students who do not like how they are served express themselves by skipping and disrupting classes. Those who like how they are served (or tolerate it) attend class and cooperate. None, however, are taught that they have a responsibility for improving the school. This is a foreign idea to them—just as it is to public school parents, teachers, and administrators. They, too, laughed at me for believing students had a responsibility to the community.

Consequently, soon after becoming a public high school administrator, I stopped asking students to take any communal responsibility. Furthermore, I did not ask this of my own children when they attended public schools. I wanted to shield them from the ridicule I received for believing such a thing.

But I must make it clear that students should not be blamed for accepting no communal responsibility. Bureaucracy prevents it. An example is the PLC literature that makes professionals responsible for improving student learning. How can students take responsibility, when they are given none?

Parents have no responsibility either. As a public high school administrator, I was frustrated by how public schools keep parents at arm's length.

The public school approach to both students and parents contrasted sharply with my high school experience. When I coached and taught in a Catholic high school, I was always available to parents because all of us were members of the same community.

At my children's public high school, though, parents are explicitly told that they need to make an appointment to talk to a coach. The public school bureaucracy puts up barriers to my involvement in my child's education because it regards me as a self-interested parent who wants to get something for my children that it cannot provide for all.

Teachers and coaches should not be blamed for this attitude either. Their relationships with parents result from the belief that they should be held accountable for student learning within bureaucratically structured schools.

The failure of public education to stand for a shared responsibility for student learning among teachers, students, and parents has devastating consequences. How much can public education improve, if parents and students share no responsibility for it?

The answer is, "hardly at all." And that has been the result as policymakers and educators try to improve public education without students and parents. Ideas like site-based decision making, standards and accountability, pay for performance, or educating the whole child do not improve public schools because students and parents do not share any improvement responsibility.

Bryk, Lee, and Holland's (1993, p. 275) descriptions of seven carefully selected Catholic high schools illustrate that everything is different in schools where "members said, 'We *are* a community,' not 'We have a *sense* of community.'" According to the authors, and my own experience, being a member of a community is at the center of a Catholic high school education. And it is this organizational difference that powerfully influences what students learn in K–12 school systems.

Bryk, Lee, and Holland (1993) described how students were counseled in the schools they studied:

> In confronting particular incidents of misconduct, the school staff discussed how the student's personal behavior had violated its norms: "You are a member of this community, and your behavior affects others." Although obeying rules was important, this was true mainly because of the larger principles the rules embodied. Responding to infractions of the rules often afforded public opportunities to teach the beliefs of the community. (p. 134)

It is a matter of course that Catholic school students have a responsibility to the community, and it is also a matter of course that teaching this responsibility is a Catholic school purpose.

Bryk, Lee, and Holland (1993) described three additional beliefs held by members of these Catholic high school communities. They are the same as the beliefs required in the alternative model. Just as public school bureaucracies are sustained by bureaucratic beliefs, Catholic high school communities are sustained by communitarian beliefs.

Admission to the Catholic high school community involved a commitment to shared beliefs and values. The authors described how community boundaries flexed with each family's decision to apply for admission:

> Indeed, the school does not operate as the principal selection mechanism; the real control rests with the students and their families through their decisions to apply for admission. The voluntary nature of this action is important, because it signifies a willingness to join the community and to accept its values. (p. 128)

Families enrolling their children in these schools implicitly agreed to what the school stood for, including a belief in community:

> For a school to operate as a community, its members (especially its adult members) must share a commitment to the community. Such a commitment requires regular public expressions of concern and action toward the common good as well as a shared understanding of the nature and importance of the common good. Such public activity is a necessary

counterbalance, we contend, to the individualistic pursuits that dominate contemporary American life. (p. 277)

A belief in the common good is a central part of Catholic school life.

According to Bryk, Lee, and Holland (1993), another belief within these high school communities was a broad definition of student achievement:

> Schools organized as communities exhibit a set of common understandings among members of the organization. These include tenets about the purpose of the school, about what students should learn, about how teachers and students should behave, and—most important—about the kind of people students are and are capable of becoming. Such educational concerns in turn reflect more fundamental beliefs about the nature of the individual and society. (p. 277)

Specifically, these Catholic high schools pursued "an emphasis on academic pursuits" (p. 132) in a context of human development that included character and spiritual development:

> Eighty-nine percent of a national sample of Catholic high school teachers supported the view that "major emphasis should be placed on mastery of reading, writing, and mathematics skills." Similar endorsements were offered for "critical thinking skills" (83 percent), "intellectual curiosity" (81 percent), and "a healthy self-concept" (89 percent). There was also substantial support for the development of "compassion" (79 percent), "tolerance" (69 percent), and a "commitment to justice" (68 percent). (pp. 134–135)

Many public schools pursued these same purposes before the standards and accountability movement forced them to focus on improving student test scores.

Compared to Catholic schools, public schools often have better facilities, better-paid teachers, more science equipment, more vocational programs, and greater financial stability. Parents of Catholic school students pay taxes to support that level of public education, but they send their children to schools on the verge of bankruptcy. Why do they do that?

The answer is simple. They believe their child's intellect, character, and spirit develop when he/she is nurtured within a community instead of a bureaucracy.

But public schools are also places where children develop—where they take risks, learn lessons, and grow. And public school teachers, administrators, and policymakers are just as devoted to the growth of young people as Catholic school personnel. I know this from experience. What is the difference between caring for students in a public school and caring for students in a Catholic one?

The difference is how each is organizationally structured. Catholic schools have no reason to exist if they are not a community. Bryk, Lee, and Holland (1993) describe how a communal structure influences the lives of Catholic high school teachers:

> Catholic school faculty typically take on multiple responsibilities: classroom teacher, coach, counselor, and adult role model. This broadly defined role creates many opportunities for faculty and student encounters. Through these social interactions, teachers convey an "intrusive interest" in students' personal lives that extends beyond the classroom door into virtually every facet of school life. In some cases it extends even to students' homes and families. In these interactions with teachers, students encounter a full person, not just a subject-matter specialist, a guidance specialist, a discipline specialist, or some other technical expert. The interaction is personal rather than bureaucratic. (p. 141)

These relationships suggest that being a member of a community is at the center of being a Catholic high school teacher and student.

According to Bryk, Lee, and Holland (1993), teaching the ideals and norms of community are also Catholic school purposes:

> They are classic institutional norms, in that they motivate and inspire human behavior toward a different world. They have the essential character of all living traditions: the ability to bring meaning to action and thereby transcend the instrumental intent of action. They represent the ideals to which the members of the community aspire, while at the same time recognizing that they may never fully achieve them. They are descriptions not of "what is" but, rather, of that toward which "we ought to be pointed." (p. 145)

Believing in these norms and ideals is essential to membership in all school communities, but they are laughed at in public schools (because they are bureaucracies).

Bryk, Lee, and Holland (1993) pointed out that these norms and ideals reflect fundamental differences between Catholic and public schools:

> Such a belief structure stands in sharp contrast to Gerald Grant's poignant description of life at Hamilton High, a comprehensive urban high school, where the major norm consists of learning how to manipulate the rule system to maximize self-interest. These beliefs are also markedly different from the portrayal offered by Sara Lawrence Lightfoot of Highland Park, an affluent suburban high school, where the primary emphasis is on individual success defined as academic achievement now in order to ensure economic success later. Intellectual values are materialistic, and school operations are distinctly bureaucratic, legalistic, and instrumental. The bonding of students to the school is weak, and there is little altruism of spirit. (p. 145)

This is not to say public schools don't teach communitarian values. They do. It is to say that community norms and values are at the center of Catholic schools, but bureaucratic norms and values are at the center of public schools. The consequences of this difference are far reaching.

Clarifications

Before examining the dysfunctional nature of the educational bureaucracy, several points need to be clarified. First, not all Catholic schools are like the ones I experienced, or the ones described by Bryk, Lee and Holland, (1993). Some are highly bureaucratic structures, themselves.

This is not surprising. The Catholic Church is one of the largest bureaucracies in the world. When the church hierarchy assumes control of a Catholic school it sometimes creates a bureaucratic structure that satisfies religious purposes more than educational ones. (This kind of Catholic school situation was mentioned in chapter 4.)

The result is that Catholic school students are indoctrinated more than educated. Indoctrination may be appropriate in elementary schools, where educational purposes are to establish foundational beliefs, knowledge, and skills; they are developmentally inappropriate at the secondary level, where school purposes are to guide adolescents as they rebel against indoctrination. My own Catholic school experiences were of this kind.

Second, Catholic schools are not the only ones in which teachers, students, and parents can say, "We *are* a community." Many non-Catholic schools are communities, too. They are also represented in this discussion of the importance of community.

A third clarification is that one type of school is not necessarily better than the other. Graduates of both Catholic and public schools have achieved great things. Catholic schools are described to illustrate the communitarian beliefs that are needed for public schools to become the *actual* communities required in the alternative model.

As long as policymakers and educators hold bureaucratic beliefs, they cannot create or sustain true school communities. That is why this chapter started with a discussion of PLCs. They promote a *sense* of community within the bureaucracy, but they are not the communities required in the alternative model. That kind of community can only be built and maintained by people whose organizational beliefs are communitarian, instead of bureaucratic.

A final clarification is that none of this makes sense until educators and parents see beneath the surface of our current schooling model. They must see that our governance and organizational beliefs are aligned. The belief that elected officials should establish educational purposes and hold educators accountable for achieving those purposes leads to a bureaucratic structure in which students are clients and teachers are bureaucratic functionaries.

A recent *Time* cover story illustrates that these relationships are difficult to see. In an article about teacher qualifications, Wallis (2008, p. 28) wrote: "Even as politicians push to hold schools and their faculty members accountable as never before for student learning, the nation faces a shortage of teaching talent."

Wallis (2008) seems not to realize that, within our current model, it is more common for political concerns to drive policymaking than it is for educational concerns to do so. In the case of the teacher talent pool, the shortage has been exacerbated by policymakers pursuing the politics of standards and accountability. If she would have seen this connection, the sentence would have started with "Because," instead of "Even as."

Her blindness was particularly apparent because she described one of her own inspirational high school teachers this way: "Dr. Cappel told us from the outset that his goal was not to prepare us for the AP biology exam; it was to teach us how to think like scientists, which he proceeded to do with a quiet passion" (p. 28).

Apparently, she did not see the connection between being inspired and the teacher's refusal to be held accountable by politicians. And she does not see the disconnection between policymakers' political purposes and the need to similarly inspire students in today's public schools.

THE DYSFUNCTION OF EDUCATIONAL BUREAUCRACY

We cannot see the dysfunction caused by our bureaucratic organizational structure because our current model makes sense at the surface. We believe students should be treated as clients, and professional educators should be held accountable for student achievement. Only by suspending these beliefs and looking beneath the surface can we see the dysfunction.

An example is how elected officials debate the specifics of NCLB. Public education pursues higher test scores, even though the shallowness of this goal is apparent to many elected officials. None are able to steer public education toward more meaningful purposes, however, because they get reelected by proclaiming their intention to hold public educators accountable for higher student test scores.

A different kind of dysfunction occurs when teacher unions achieve more political power than citizens. In these situations, elected officials need teacher votes to be reelected, so they put teacher interests before those of students and parents.

The dysfunction is that elected officials have to accommodate the professionals they are supposed to hold accountable. And teachers often respond by obeying elected officials for no other reason than their teacher unions helped get them elected. Students are the ones who suffer, which is the same point documented by Williams (2005).

COMMUNITIES OF INCLUSION, NOT EXCLUSION

The alternative model requires the establishment of *actual* public school communities. In order to understand what these look like, a distinction must be made between communities of inclusion and communities of exclusion. According to Peck (1987), inclusive communities are formed by people who come together and accept each other's differences, but exclusive communities are formed by rejecting those who do not share certain commonalities.

Without this distinction, country clubs would be considered the kind of community required in the alternative model. They are not. With annual membership dues in the thousands of dollars, clubs of this type are designed to be communities of exclusion.

Catholic schools might be considered communities of exclusion too. They are exclusive because many families cannot afford tuition payments, despite need-based scholarships and sliding tuition scales. My experience is that they are communities of inclusion, even though they are not as inclusive as they desire. Catholic schools keep tuition as low as possible in order to be as inclusive as possible. The result is that many of them teeter on the verge of financial collapse, which is the price they pay for being as inclusive as possible.

My experience as a small-town public high school administrator also taught me about communities of inclusion and exclusion. All three of my public high school experiences were in small, rural communities that exhibited the sense of community typically associated with small-town America. But my experiences in these towns were different from my Catholic school experiences in two ways.

The first is that they were communities of exclusion more than inclusion. People who moved in from elsewhere were welcome; but they would always be outsiders. This may be human nature, but both Peck (1987) and I believe it is part of our uneducated human nature—the nature we overcome as we become educated.

The second difference is that these school systems were bureaucracies, so they lacked the kind of community found in Catholic schools. Even though local property taxes funded the schools, persons structured the schools in a bureaucratic hierarchy because they did not trust each other enough to form a true community.

Again, a distinction is made between *being* a community and having a *sense* of community. These school districts had a sense of community, but they were not inclusive enough to be the type of community required in the alternative model.

CONCLUSION

Much of this chapter is based on Bryk, Lee, and Holland's (1993) study of seven Catholic high schools. Their book is the only one in which education scholars distinguish between being a community and having a sense of community. This distinction captures the fundamental difference between my Catholic and public school experiences. It also captures the difference between our current model's organizational structure and the one required in the alternative model.

This chapter explored relationships and beliefs that are beneath the surface. Bureaucratic beliefs lead to bureaucratic structures, and these beliefs and structures prevent the establishment of actual community. On the other hand, inclusive Catholic school communities are examples of what is required in the alternative model. All community members, not just professionals, share the responsibility for improving student learning and maintaining the community.

One reason public education is impervious to change and improvement is the belief that public education must be structured bureaucratically. Only when this belief is suspended can persons build school communities in which students thrive and develop the six virtues of the educated person.

Another reason public education is impervious to improvement is the topic of the next chapter. Our current model takes a social scientific approach to improving schools. If school improvement is more art than social science, shouldn't our improvement paradigm be aesthetic? The next chapter explores this question.

8

AN AESTHETIC SCHOOL
IMPROVEMENT PARADIGM

After presentations from a panel of scholars at the 1989 American Educational Research Association (AERA) conference, a public school teacher stood up and said, "This conference is like a meeting of the AMA [American Medical Association] without a single physician in attendance." Judging by the nodding in agreement around me, the analogy seemed accurate and disturbing to many of us. The panelists responded by agreeing that educational researchers should work more closely with teachers.

Many educators and policymakers believe improving education is like improving the practice of medicine. Sarason (1990, p. 118) noted, "No less than in medicine, many efforts at educational reform are justified on the basis of research studies." He went on to make the point that the medical analogy "does not hold":

> If these studies were not experimental in methodology (for example, no comparison groups, no before or after measures, no "hard" data), it said less about the researchers' devotion to the canons of science and the rules of evidence than it did about what one is realistically up against in conducting research in education. In this respect, the imagery of white-coated researchers working in instrument-filled, encapsulated laboratories does not hold for the curriculum researchers. (p. 118)

Should educators and policymakers adopt the medical analogy, as suggested at the AERA, or should they reject it because it "does not hold"?

REJECTING THE MEDICAL FIELD ANALOGY

Sarason (1990) believes in research, but he admonishes educators and policymakers to recognize its limitations and not overpromise results. Few have heeded his admonition.

No Child Left Behind uses the medical research model as the definition for "research-based" instructional programs. Apparently, federal policymakers believe the findings of studies that mimic medical science will enable teachers to bring all students to grade level by 2014—the greatest overpromise of all time.

I used to believe principals and teachers improve schools by applying educational research in their classrooms, just as physicians apply medical research to the treatment of patients. That was before I took a group of educational administration graduate students to the 1996 Qualitative Interest Group (QUIG) research conference at the University of Georgia.

After attending several paper presentations, my students were drowning in academic debate. They knew that esoteric research topics, discussed in tortured language, had nothing to do with improving schools. They scorned my idea of a "field trip," but they articulated it only by looking at each other and rolling their eyes. Today I thank them for trying to hide their disgust, but most of all I thank them for being disgusted.

They were disgusted because they were devoted to making a positive difference in the lives of students and teachers, and they knew these academic debates were irrelevant to their work in schools. Their reaction caused me to challenge both the medical field analogy and the social science improvement paradigm.

Many social scientists have challenged the medical field analogy too. As early as the 1930s, Lyon, Lubin, Meriam, and Wright (1931) argued that we know the natural world differently from the way we know the social world. Educators and policymakers have responded to this distinction by seeing education as an applied social science. The result is a social scientific improvement paradigm for education. It is time to challenge this idea too.

REJECTING THE SOCIAL SCIENCE IMPROVEMENT PARADIGM

Policymakers and educators believe schools improve by applying the findings of educational (social scientific) research to school situations. Thousands of books and journal articles describe educational "best practices" because the social science improvement paradigm assumes educational research findings can indicate which practices are more effective than others. It is believed that appropriately applying these findings in schools leads to improved teaching and learning.

But philosophers like MacIntyre (1981), Bates (1984), Greenfield (1986), and Kneller (1994) challenge the epistemological assumptions of the social sciences. MacIntyre (1981) explained his objection to the social science of management this way:

> The claim that the manager makes to effectiveness rests of course on the further claim to possess a stock of knowledge by means of which organizations and social structures can be moulded. Such knowledge would have to include a set of factual law-like generalisations which would enable the manager to predict that, if an event or state of affairs of a certain type were to occur or to be brought about, some other event or state of affairs of some specific kind would result. For only such law-like generalisations could yield those particular causal explanations and predictions by means of which the manager could mould, influence and control the social environment. (p. 74)

Because there are no such lawlike generalizations that explain cause and effect in the social environment, MacIntyre (1981, p. 72) concluded that managerial effectiveness is "a masquerade of social control rather than a reality." For the same reason, educational effectiveness is also a masquerade. (This metaphor is explained later in the chapter.)

Philosophers like MacIntyre (1981) and Kneller (1994), and psychologists like Sarason (1990), say a science of education should be rejected, or at least tempered. So why do federal policymakers require that education programs be "research based"?

Apparently, the advances made by *natural* science research entice them to believe *social* science research can achieve similar advances in education. This belief dominates our current model of education, even though educational research has done little to advance public education. It is time to put an end to both the medical analogy and the social science improvement paradigm.

The next section describes how we regard the natural sciences. The one after that describes the differences between the natural and social sciences. The fifth section of this chapter explains why the social science paradigm does not improve education. The sixth section explains why we must reject the social science improvement paradigm. And the last section describes the aesthetic improvement paradigm of the alternative model.

Chapter 1 defined "paradigm" as "the general set of assumptions, questions, and methods that structures a field of inquiry at any given time" (Calhoun, 2002). The following sections describe three paradigms by discussing their underlying assumptions, the types of questions they ask, the methods they use to study those questions, and the kinds of knowledge that result.

Before illustrating and discussing these paradigms, it should be noted that the following figures and descriptions do not represent the complex ways scientists and philosophers think about the sciences and the arts. Instead, they highlight the differences among three sets of paradigmatic assumptions, questions, methods, and knowledge. Figures 8.1 and 8.2 illustrate scientific paradigms. Figure 8.3 illustrates an aesthetic one.

THE NATURAL SCIENCE PARADIGM

Figure 8.1 depicts the natural science paradigm. The laws of nature are represented by the lines within the circle. An example is that water vaporizes at 100 degrees Celsius.

The longer lines close to the perimeter represent the more complex discoveries built on the more fundamental ones, represented by the shorter lines close to the center. For example, video recording was made

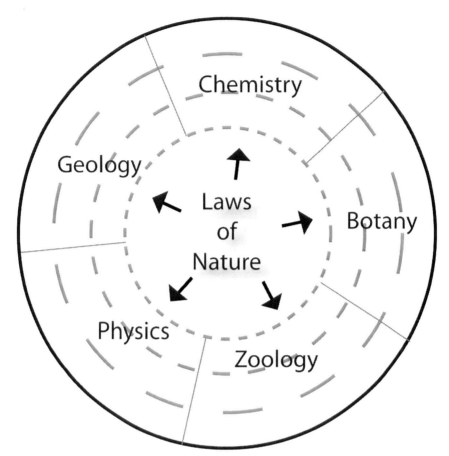

Figure 8.1.   The Natural Science Paradigm Neil Torda

possible by audio recording discoveries. The world is continually being shaped by the application of natural science discoveries to the development of new technologies.

Although the natural science disciplines are interconnected, schools teach that they are separate. High school chemistry is separate from botany, which is separate from physics. The lines between the disciplines represent this fragmentation.

An assumption of the natural science paradigm is that the physical world is governed by laws of nature. Scientists enhance their understanding of the natural world by discovering these laws.

A second assumption is that natural science discoveries have been a driver of human evolution. Historians often reference the technological advances that have altered the human condition. Nomadic societies became agrarian through the development of new technologies. Those societies evolved into the industrial societies of the 19th and 20th centuries and the knowledge-based societies of today, and these developments favor the strong and adaptive over the weak and maladaptive.

The first type of question asked by natural scientists concerns the laws of nature: What are they? How do they work? The scientific method is used to generate findings. A laboratory result becomes a law when the same result is produced each time the experiment is replicated. Scientists build an understanding of causation in the natural world through these laboratory experiments.

As natural laws and causes are discovered, a second type of question is asked: "How can these discoveries improve the human condition?" Laboratory experiments are part of the natural world, so natural science findings can be directly applied to the natural world. All that is needed is for scientists to have enough imagination to envision new applications.

In the language of the six virtues, advances in natural science knowledge emerge from both *understanding* and *imagination*. Understanding is developed in the laboratory and imagination is used to apply it in ways that shape the environment and improve the conditions for human life. Technologies that can only be imagined today will take us down a path that continues to improve the environment—or so we believe.

THE SOCIAL SCIENCE PARADIGM

Figure 8.2 depicts the social science paradigm. The center circle is the world of lived experience. Just as the natural sciences describe the natural world, the social sciences describe the world of human experience.

An assumption of the social science paradigm is that research findings explain what is more or less effective. This is represented outside the circle, where social science disciplines claim to have found what is more or less effective in the world of human experience. To understand this paradigm, we must understand the concept of "effectiveness." What does it mean to say something is "effective"?

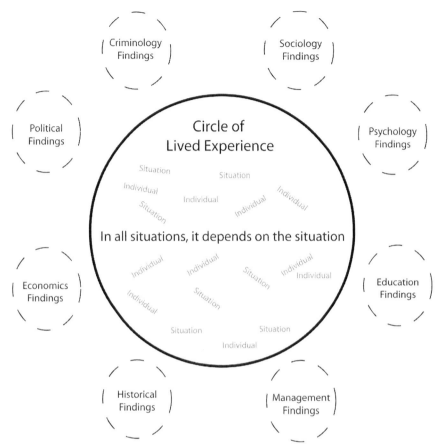

Figure 8.2.   The Social Science Paradigm Neil Torda

I remember writing a graduate school paper in which I wanted to claim a specific administrative approach was desirable. I could defend my claim by either writing a paragraph that provided a rationale or by citing corroborating research findings. The problem was that both approaches required more effort than they were worth because the claim I wanted to make was a minor one. I was about to eliminate the claim altogether, when the right word occurred to me. If I simply said the approach was "effective," it could not be challenged.

I put "effective" in the sentence, and it worked. It read something like, "Group decision making is an effective way to cultivate collegial school cultures." Who could argue with that? Certainly group decision making cultivates collegiality in some way or another. If this claim were challenged, I could point to at least one way in which the action or decision achieved a desired result; and there it was—"effectiveness." I remember this situation not only because I found a good way to complete my paper without writing an extra paragraph or going to the library but also because I discovered the emptiness of "effectiveness."

Sergiovanni described a similar discovery in an interview with Ron Brandt (1992). When asked what caused him to rethink his ideas about leadership, he said:

> Well, frankly, much of my work on leadership over the years has been more a part of the problem than the solution. When I recognized that, I began to rethink traditional management theory. It came about gradually, of course, but I particularly remember doing a workshop on leadership styles somewhere in the Philippines. We had an instrument and so on, and I would say that to be effective in a certain situation the leader should do such and such. And every time I'd say that one person would ask, "What do you mean by effective?" He was a pain in the neck for the whole two days, so I put him down and ignored him—but that has haunted me ever since.
>
> I began to feel that what I had been saying was vacuous. . . .
>
> So I began a different line of inquiry. About 1982 or '83, it became clear to me that while my students and people in workshops were patient and respectful of what I had to say, they actually made a distinction between workshop knowledge and real life career knowledge. In real life they weren't driven by the theories I taught them, but by other ideas and other conceptions. (p. 47)

Because of this experience, Sergiovanni ignores the social science dimensions of leadership in favor of the moral dimensions.

The irony is that, although effectiveness claims are the ultimate for social science researchers, they have little meaning in the real world. Claims of effectiveness can be made for almost anything. Research can be cited to support the effectiveness of phonics or whole language, traditional math or integrated math, student-centered classrooms or teacher-centered ones.

Because "effective" can be defined in relationship to any desired outcome, of which there are always many, effectiveness is "a masquerade of social control rather than a reality" (MacIntyre, 1981, p. 72). Like a mask, it hides reality as it gives the appearance of something unique and fascinating. The person in Sergiovanni's workshop asked, "What do you mean by effective?" because he wanted to see the reality behind the mask. Sergiovanni could not answer him because "effectiveness" was whatever the studies defined it to be.

A second assumption of the social science paradigm is that research findings explain human behavior causes and effects. Similar to the biological and chemical causalities that tell medical doctors which drugs to prescribe, some social science findings are assumed to tell educators which remedies to apply in schools.

This is the idea of applying theory to practice discussed in chapter 2. Although applying educational theory to practice has not improved public education, a belief that it does persists and is promoted throughout the literature. For example, "Educator Use of Research to Improve Practice" is the title of a 2004 ASCD research brief (Author, 2004).

Interestingly, the fourth question explored in this publication is "Do medical practitioners make greater use of research findings than educators, and if so, why?" Both the medical field analogy and the assumption that theory should be applied to practice are alive and well within the social science improvement paradigm.

The social sciences explore questions about the economics, psychology, sociology, anthropology, politics, and so forth of the human condition. As social science disciplines mature, their explanations become more qualified and more interdisciplinary (Wheatley, 2007). Figure 8.2 represents this in the dotted lines surrounding the disciplines, suggesting that disciplinary borders are open and fluid.

To study questions about human experience, social scientists use methods that are both quantitative and qualitative. Methodological debates have gone on for decades because each methodology is based on a different epistemology.

Quantitative studies are based on an epistemology that mirrors the natural science way of knowing. Studies are designed to determine what happens to a single, dependent variable when independent variables are controlled and manipulated. Studies of this kind are "quantitative" because researchers use statistical techniques to control variables and to understand results. Quantitative studies result in the following kind of knowledge: "All other things being equal, when x is applied to the situation, y is the result."

The results of quantitative studies can be generalized to all other identical situations. This concept is captured in the phrase "All other things being equal."

Qualitative studies do not control variables or use statistical principles to understand results. The researcher is the instrument through which data are gathered and interpreted. Findings cannot be generalized to other situations because controls are not used to isolate and study variable interactions.

Qualitative studies result in a different kind of knowledge than that obtained from quantitative studies. They generate knowledge about the specific situation that is studied. This knowledge informs the judgment that is needed to interpret and apply findings to other situations. Those who question the value of these studies point out that, after they are completed, educators are in the same position they were in before the study was completed—needing to use imagination and judgment to address their actual situations.

Having to rely on judgment and imagination is considered regrettable within the social science improvement paradigm. In the language of the six virtues, this paradigm values and promotes *understanding*, but it devalues *imagination*. Examples run throughout the social science literature.

Educational time-on-task studies, for example, have found that, all other things being equal, the more time spent learning a task, the greater the learning. Within the social science paradigm, this finding is valued. Outside this paradigm, people who engage their imaginations don't need a single study to inform them of this correlation.

Another example can be found in Emmons' book (2007, p.3), which "showcases the new science of gratitude":

> We discovered scientific proof that when people regularly engage in the systematic cultivation of gratitude, they experience a variety of measurable benefits: psychological, physical, and interpersonal. The evidence on gratitude contradicts the widely held view that all people have a "set point" of happiness that cannot be reset by any known means: in some cases, people have reported that gratitude led to transformative life changes. And, even more important, the family, friends, partners, and others that surround them consistently report that people who practice gratitude seem measurably happier and are more pleasant to be around. (p. 3)

Again, only the most unimaginative person needs a science of gratitude to realize that, all other things being equal, grateful people are better companions than ingrates.

Ironically, a third example can be found in Pink's book (2006) about the value of imaginative thinking:

> Although it is relatively new, the JSPE [Jefferson Scale of Physician Empathy] has produced some intriguing results. For example, high scores on the Empathy test generally correlated with high marks on clinical care. That is, all other things being equal, a patient was more likely to get better with an empathic doctor than with a detached one. (p. 170)

This may be an "intriguing" finding to a social scientist, but it is hardly "intriguing" to those who can imagine the difference between being treated by an empathic physician and an unfeeling one.

The key concept in all three examples is "all other things being equal." Social scientists cannot control the environment; so their findings are always based on the theoretical premise that all other things are equal. The irony is stunning. We can imagine situations in which "all other things are equal," but we can never experience them because all other things are *never* equal. A situation that can only be imagined is the foundation for a paradigm that devalues imagination.

Some might say this is a straw man argument—I am exaggerating the claims of social science to make them look ridiculous. Am I exaggerating?

Do the reports of social science research adequately describe the limitations of their findings? Do they explain that findings are true in theory only, that results can only be applied to situations in which all other things are equal, or that all other things are never equal? If they did, educators and policymakers would value imaginative ways to improve education more than those based on research findings.

DIFFERENCES BETWEEN THE NATURAL AND SOCIAL SCIENCES

The two scientific paradigms are based on different assumptions. They ask different questions, use different methods, and produce different kinds of knowledge. These differences should cause us to question whether social science discoveries advance the human condition in the same way natural science discoveries advance our ability to shape the natural world. The differences are evident in a comparison of figure 8.1 with figure 8.2.

One difference is that the natural science disciplines are inside the circle of nature, but social science disciplines are outside the world of lived experience. Human life is experienced in the relationship between a person and a situation. This idea is expressed inside the circle of lived experience with the statement "In all situations, it depends on the situation."

I discovered this truth by doing role-plays with my graduate students. They would play the principal and I would play antagonists in hypothetical situations written for class. No matter how thoughtfully they played the principal, I played antagonists in ways that prevented them from solving the problems.

I did this because, if they did not have a problem, there was no reason to play out the situation. I told students they would not be able to solve the problems, which was my way of warning them not to regard their performance as a reflection of their administrative abilities.

After class one night, I sensed that students were disregarding the warning. Several seemed genuinely disappointed in their performances. I had to find a better explanation for why their role-playing performance was unrelated to their actual abilities.

As I drove home I realized that, in real-school situations, principals know more than what can be described in a written scenario. They know about the history of the organization and about its people—their values, norms, and beliefs. All this background knowledge is the context of real-life situations, but role-players had none of it in a two-page description.

A better explanation of why role-playing was unrelated to their actual abilities was that what they did *not* know was infinitely greater than what they did know. That was why I could always play antagonists with knowledge they did not have; and that is why I could always make the situation impossible for them to solve. When I realized this, it occurred to me that I was being unfair, and I started to think that I should play antagonists within the boundaries of what was in the written scenarios,

At that point, the obvious struck me. Principals are always in situations in which what they don't know is greater than what they know. What I considered unfair is exactly what principals experience all the time. No matter how much principals know about a situation, the unknown is always infinitely greater and infinitely more important. Instead of being unfair, it is realistic to play antagonists with knowledge principals do not have and cannot have.

In the world of lived experience, no psychological, sociological, political, management, economic, or educational explanation is truer than, "In all situations, it depends on the situation." That is why social science findings cannot penetrate the circle of lived experience. Unlike natural science results, social science findings are theoretically true, but whether they are true in a specific, lived situation is unknowable.

For example, right now you are reading this sentence. It is your lived experience, the cause of which, and the effects of which, depend on you and your specific situation. The social sciences provide psychological, sociological, economic, or educational explanations of these causes and effects, but they are not your experience. They refer to your experience from perspectives that ring the circle of lived experience, but they cannot penetrate the circle because taking a social science finding into the circle of lived experience strips it of the theoretical condition that makes it true—it is only true in all situations in which all other things are equal. The truth of any social science finding in the world of lived experience is unknowable because no two lived situations are the same.

The application of social science findings must be mediated by an imaginative understanding of situational factors. This difference is discussed in greater depth elsewhere in this chapter.

A second difference between the natural and social science paradigms is that the natural sciences produce advanced knowledge by building on the knowledge gained from more fundamental laws. The aforementioned truth about lived human experience prevents this from happening in the social sciences.

Human life is not experienced as a series of situations in which discoveries from prior experience can be applied to subsequent ones. The application of prior learning and experience is always mediated by human judgment, which involves both understanding and imagination. We can never know to what extent prior learning and experience are relevant to subsequent situations because every situation is different from every other situation.

Before leaving the social science paradigm, this critique needs to be qualified. Like the findings of natural science research, social science findings promote *understanding*. This is good because the virtue of understanding is developed and enhanced through social science research. Insofar as the understanding of social science research devalues *imagination*, however, it comes at a great cost to the possibilities for improving schools.

This is analogous to situations in which golfers read instructional articles to improve their swing. This is a good thing. Right? Greater understanding leads to improvement, doesn't it? Or, at least, it causes no harm.

My experience has been that a focus on *understanding* can be harmful. Often my golf game is worsened by reading instructional articles because their main effect is to distract me from the concentration needed to perform my natural swing. When I try to integrate a new understanding about a "proper" swing, I am distracted from the fundamentals that produce my own natural swing. The fundamentals are maintaining my balance while swinging the club along a line that hits the ball toward the target.

My hypothesis is that, if every golf instructional article said nothing more than "Stay balanced as you swing the club along a line that hits the ball toward the hole," the effect on the quality of golf would be more positive than the results that have been attained from our current situation, in which instructional articles cover every aspect of the golf swing—the proper grip, take away, weight shift, swing path, shoulder turn, and so on.

The corresponding educational hypothesis is that education would be more improved if every school improvement article said nothing other than "Use imagination as you apply understanding, strong character, courage, humility, and generosity to situations you want to improve."

In summary, the social science paradigm assumes research findings inform educators about what is more or less effective. It uses both quantitative and qualitative methods to explore questions about the causes and effects of human thought and behavior. Its findings result in specific, objective knowledge about a single variable, or more general, subjective knowledge about specific situations. It promotes understanding but not imagination because it fails to question the limitations of its findings, even though those limitations are easily imagined.

If the social science paradigm is based on the false assumption that it informs practitioners about effectiveness, if it answers questions that ignore the fundamental truth that "in all situations it depends on the situation," and if it produces correlation findings that are easily imagined—maybe the reason schools do not improve is that our improvement paradigm is the wrong one. The next two sections discuss that possibility before offering an alternative.

THE SOCIAL SCIENCE PARADIGM DOES NOT IMPROVE EDUCATION

One of the reasons social science research findings do not improve schools was mentioned earlier. Their findings cannot be directly applied to school situations with any confidence that they will improve the situation.

We have a long history of trying to identify and duplicate "effective" programs across classrooms, schools, and districts. The National Diffusion Network was established in 1974, and the New American Schools Development Corporation was established in 1991; both were created to promote the duplication of supposedly "effective" programs. These efforts continue.

According to Bell (1993),

> The next iteration of school reform initiatives was the President's education strategy, known as America 2000. The centerpiece of this strategy was the design of new models of schools and their installation in 535 sites across the nation. The lofty aim was to have these new schools up and running and being duplicated throughout the U.S. by the year 2000. . . . The original plan had been to find 25 to 30 design teams for these "break-the-mold" schools, but the number was subsequently reduced to 11. These design teams are now at work, and the education world is looking for their first reports to emerge on the scene any day. (p. 594)

The reports have come and gone, with little effect on American public education.

More recently we have books about getting results (Schmoker, 1996, 2006) and what works in schools (Marzano, 2003). These publications promote the adoption of successful programming in new situations. Does this improve education?

The "adopt what is effective" concept promotes the duplication of instructional materials and methods. The most essential aspects of all learning situations, however, are not the materials or methods but the relationships between the learner and the situation and between the learner and the teacher. These relationships can never be transferred from one situation to another.

Some might argue that, even if research findings cannot be applied directly, they are valuable because they inform understanding, which is the first step toward improvement. They might argue that being more effective is a desirable outcome in an area that needs improving, and social science findings help educators and policymakers address those areas.

In fact, this is exactly what happens within the social science improvement paradigm. And this is the second reason the social science paradigm does not improve schools. Educational researchers study an endless variety of ways to improve schools because effectiveness can be defined as desirable outcomes in any number of areas that need improving. In the absence of a clear, agreed-upon definition of what it means to be educated, however, pursuing these outcomes takes us toward the periphery of education, and away from its essence.

For example, schools have been directed to improve standardized test scores, close achievement gaps, and prepare students for a global economy. These purposes are laudable, but they distract educators and policymakers from asking and defining what it means to be educated.

The introduction discussed the importance of sticking to the essence. A basketball analogy was used to explain that the best coaches reinforce the simplest, most essential basketball strategies. This idea extends to the best teachers too. They work from a simple, fundamental definition of what it means to be educated, and they nudge students toward it. My graduate students were drowning in academic debate at the University of Georgia QUIG conference because their teaching is grounded in what is simple and essential, not what is complex and peripheral.

Within our current model, educators teach understanding, strong character, and generosity. But they also ignore imagination, courage, and humility, thereby teaching intellectual incompetence, fear, and pride. All of this goes unnoticed because the social science paradigm distracts us from the philosophical question of what it means to be educated as it focuses educators and policymakers on what is effective at achieving uninspiring, shallow, and peripheral purposes. The educational results match perfectly.

WE MUST REJECT THE SOCIAL STUDIES IMPROVEMENT PARADIGM

Assuming imaginative educators and policymakers are ready to improve schools, what needs to happen? The first step is to reject the social science paradigm for improving schools. This section explains why this is necessary. (It foreshadows chapter 9, which describes how we can move from our current schooling model to the alternative.)

The first reason to reject this paradigm is that it does not address the essential question of what it means to be educated. Logic suggests that, without a clear definition of what we are trying to accomplish, schools are unlikely to accomplish it. Logic suggests that the opposite is also true, too—teaching and schooling are likely to improve when purposes are clear.

Recent history provides an example. Since improved schools have been defined as those with improved test scores, test scores have improved (Cavanagh, 2008). When it comes to improving education, a clear definition of purpose almost ensures its achievement.

Has American public education ever had a clear definition of what it means to be educated? If it did, how was it pushed aside by a definition that focuses on improving standardized test scores? We have a vacuum waiting to be filled by an inspiring definition of what it means to be educated. Establishing such a definition requires philosophical thought and discussion, not more research.

The second reason to reject the social science paradigm is that it is based on a dysfunctional relationship. Sarason (1990) described the relationship problems at the heart of our current paradigm:

> University faculty generally consider themselves superior to school personnel in terms of understanding issues, problems, and courses of action,

and in intellectual leadership. It is a stance of superiority that they, wittingly or unwittingly, communicate quite effectively to school personnel, who do nothing to dispute it because they cannot afford to. It is a stance fed by disdain for the performance of school personnel.

The symbiotic relationship between schools and the university is marked by strong ambivalence. School personnel often derogate the quality and relevance of their professional education, and the university faculty look upon the poor quality of our schools as in large measure due to the poor intellectual and personal qualities of school personnel. (p. 66)

To say these relationships are unlikely to improve schools is an understatement.

Although the social science improvement paradigm assumes researchers and teachers share school improvement responsibilities, this arrangement has yielded little improvement. The responsibility for school improvement should be shared among school personnel, local policymakers, parents, and students.

For me, the most fulfilling part of teaching in a Catholic high school was sharing the improvement responsibility with other members of the community. My faculty colleagues and I often talked with each other, our students, and their parents about our shared commitment to the growth of students and to the betterment of the school and the world.

As a public high school assistant principal, I also shared struggles and commitments with faculty colleagues, but the results were not the same. Our commitment to improving the school was tempered by being employees of a school board that believed school improvement started with educational research.

The emptiness of this belief struck me during my first public school in-service day. I had never heard the term "in-service" in Catholic schools, so I searched for its meaning as I walked around my public high school that day.

I was frustrated by what I found. Many teachers expressed negative attitudes both during and after in-service activities. They complained about boring, irrelevant presentations made by outsiders who knew little about their situations or specific issues.

My second frustration came from believing we needed time to do what I did as a Catholic school faculty member. We needed time to talk among ourselves, but in-service days took time that could have been devoted to those conversations.

The public school idea of in-service is based on the belief that school improvement is the shared responsibility of teachers and educational researchers. In spite of this belief, teachers and principals know that research findings are mostly irrelevant to their work. Some of them realize that members of the school community are the only ones who can both *understand* what to do and *imagine* how to do it. And some of them also realize that research findings distract them from that responsibility.

That is why Bellamy and Goodlad (2008) described the benefits that accrue to schools with an inward focus:

> These organizations have focused on the local processes through which school goals are negotiated, school character is determined, and school programs are prioritized. . . .
>
> This approach reflects both a measure of pessimism about remotely controlled reform and a belief that schools are more like gardens than machines: they are never "fixed" once and for all. Every community brings its own combinations of student aspirations, family expectations, teachers and educational leaders, businesses that see commercial opportunities in schools, and employers who hope for particular kinds of graduates. And every community has its own level of willingness to pay for basics and extras. Interaction involving this mix of people and interests create the schools we have now, and renewal of those schools similarly depends on how local people and institutions interact in the future. Schools require constant minding, and they thrive in proportion to the quality of this local attention. (p. 567)

Members of the school community are responsible for this work, not researchers from the university.

School improvement is more likely when local policymakers and school personnel reject the social science improvement paradigm because only then will they be able to engage in the philosophical discussions needed to agree on what it means to be educated. And only then will they be able to adopt the improvement paradigm required in the alternative model.

AN AESTHETIC SCHOOL IMPROVEMENT PARADIGM

An aesthetic improvement paradigm is the fifth element of the alternative model. It frames human experience in terms of appreciation instead of effectiveness. Works of art are appreciated as expressions of what is more or less beautiful about the world and the human condition. Artists invite audiences to interact with and appreciate their work for what it expresses about both personal experience and human life in general.

Americans are typically well-versed in the arts of music, movies, literature, photography, drama, painting, and sculpture. Do our aesthetic sensibilities extend to teaching and schooling? Do we see them as expressions of what is more or less beautiful about human life and the human condition? Imagination and creativity are powerful forces in education, just as they are in all the arts.

Much has been written about the art of teaching. Highet's (1989) work is a classic, and many educational treatises make the point that teaching is an art. If teaching is widely viewed as an art, why have we not adopted an aesthetic paradigm (rather than a social scientific one) for improving schools?

The Art and Science of Teaching (Marzano, 2007) provides an answer. The following paragraph from the introduction describes the art of teaching:

> In short, research will never be able to identify instructional strategies that work with every student in every class. The best research can do is tell us which strategies have a good chance (i.e., high probability) of working well with students. Individual classroom teachers must determine which strategies to employ with the right students at the right time. In effect, a good part of effective teaching is an art—hence the title, *The Art and Science of Teaching*. (p. 5)

It seems Marzano (2007) believes that "in all situations, it depends on the situation." And he writes that "effective teaching is an art." Throughout the rest of the book, however, he describes what is more or less "effective" and never discusses what is more or less appreciated or beautiful.

In other words, like others who work within our current schooling model, Marzano frames the aesthetic essence of teaching with the social science paradigm. Social science research is cited throughout, and when research fails to provide unequivocal support and guidance, Marzano (2007) regards this as unfortunate but highly relevant to school personnel who want to improve education.

If the art of teaching were framed by an aesthetic paradigm, a lack of research guidance would be of no relevance, just as it is of no relevance to musicians, filmmakers, actors, painters, playwrights, and so forth. It is simple. Teaching is an art, so the improvement of teaching and schooling should be framed by an aesthetic paradigm that focuses on appreciation and being appreciated.

Figure 8.3 zooms in on the school improvement element of the alternative model.

Figure 8.3.   An Aesthetic School Improvement Paradigm Neil Torda

The underlying assumption of this improvement paradigm is that teaching and learning are art forms. Like all arts, they express an appreciation for what is more or less beautiful about the world and the human condition. More specifically, they are expressions of what is more or less beautiful about human growth and development. Adult appreciation of students is expressed in the modeling and teaching of understanding, imagination, strength, courage, humility, and generosity. Student appreciation of adult modeling and teaching is expressed in the development of these virtues.

Although we are fond of saying "Beauty is in the eye of the beholder," when it comes to teaching and schooling, this is not true. Within an aesthetic school improvement paradigm, the virtue capacities of understanding, character strength, and humility—and their expressions in imaginative, courageous, and generous behavior—are always beautiful. On the other hand, the vices of ignorance, weakness, and pride—and their expressions in unimaginative, fearful, and selfish behavior—are always ugly.

At its most fundamental level, life is experienced as that which is more or less beautiful. As I explained elsewhere (Hurley, 2002, p. 25), "our sense of aesthetics permeates our lives. It is fundamental and basic to human nature, not something reserved for those with extensive cultural experiences and sensitivities."

For example, when shoppers rifle through racks of clothing, their sense of aesthetics is guiding their purchase decisions. Similarly, our sense of aesthetics causes our heads to turn to admire the shape of a passing automobile.

Learning situations are also concerned with what is more or less beautiful. Since my youngest boy was three, I have pitched baseballs to him and he has improved his batting skills. These have been beautiful experiences for both of us. I enjoy the beauty of his swing, and he enjoys the beautiful feel of hitting a line drive.

Some of our recent sessions have turned ugly. As a fifteen-year-old boy, he has a lot of pride. Therefore, he gets angry when he does not hit well, and his anger makes his hitting worse, which causes more anger.

I wanted to find a way to make these experiences beautiful again, so I wondered if I should teach him about better hitting technique, about the ugliness I was experiencing as his father, or about his present stage of adolescent development. I could use kinesthetic theories, Freud's theories, educational theories, or even economic theories because he wants to earn a college scholarship.

None of these approaches, however, would have addressed the most fundamental way these sessions were being experienced. A once beautiful experience had become ugly, and pride was the cause. When my son failed to hit like he "thought" he could, his pride was expressed in anger, and his performance and attitude became ugly. Anyone who watched us could see the ugliness, even if they knew nothing about his skills, his psychological development, or our relationship.

The most fundamental approach to addressing what had become ugly was for me to teach the humility that makes athletic success beautiful. All successful athletes "know" they are good. They don't "think" it, they "know" it to their core. When this deep knowledge is tempered by the other aspects of humility, the result is a beautiful performance by a skilled athlete.

In order for what was ugly to become beautiful again, I had to teach my son to have more humility and less pride. When I told him that in the middle of one of our ugly sessions, he said, "That isn't it. I am angry because I think I can hit better."

I replied, "That is the problem. You have to "*know* you can hit better, not *think* it." Of course this made him angrier (probably because I expressed it with more pride than humility).

A few days after this exchange, he described one of his at-bats this way: "You were right—I hate it when you are right—I went up there and forgot about everything. I knew I could get a hit."

The result was beautiful, both because of the line drive and because of the humility that is developing. When my son "knows" he can hit, he can better accept his failures. All good hitters possess this kind of knowledge and demonstrate this kind of acceptance.

Even the learning of an athletic skill requires an approach that is focused more on what is beautiful and ugly than what is physical, psychological, sociological, or economic. The most fundamental approach is one that asks, "Why is this ugly? How can it become beautiful?" In learning situations, the answer is always the same—the development and expression of the six virtues makes learning beautiful, and expressions of the six vices make it ugly. The power of the aesthetic improvement paradigm is its simplicity and universality.

The methods of the aesthetic school improvement paradigm, like those of other art forms, emerge from imagination. The more imaginative an artist's methods and the more those methods connect with audience imaginations, the greater the aesthetic experience. In the case of teaching and learning, the more the teacher's imagination connects with the learner's, the more beautiful the learning situation and the greater the learning.

Similarly, the knowledge generated by an aesthetic paradigm for improving education is like the knowledge generated from experiencing the arts. When we are moved by what is painted, photographed, or played out on stage, we gain knowledge about human life. By appreciating the artist's expression, we learn about our own specific situations and the human condition in general.

For example, photographs of Nazi concentration camp inmates express the ugliness that is part of human experience. The barbed wire and the emaciated figures capture man's inhumanity to man. These images are appreciated as expressions of human cruelty.

An aesthetic school improvement paradigm promotes all aspects of appreciation—all the way from appreciating the ugliness of human cruelty to appreciating the beauty of the world around us. Teachers who model the six virtues promote the development of appreciation as they invite students to see and experience the beauty of an educated person. This is the first step toward being educated themselves.

In summary, an aesthetic paradigm assumes school improvement is an art. It assumes schools improve when teachers and principals express their understanding, strong character, and humility, as they act with imagination, courage, and generosity. This paradigm addresses questions about what is more or less beautiful. Its methods are any that can be imagined as educators connect with students and engage them in appreciating what it means to be an educated person.

9

FROM OUR CURRENT MODEL TO THE ALTERNATIVE

Figure 1.1 illustrates relationships among the five elements of our current schooling model. A brief review is needed before discussing how to replace it with the alternative.

Americans believe in the desirability of democratic governance, so public education is democratically governed. Elected officials establish educational purposes and hire administrators to supervise teachers. All three groups (elected officials, administrators, and teachers) believe educational research findings should guide the improvement of teaching and schooling.

Chapter 3 presented an alternative model in which purpose precedes governance, and the five elements take different forms.

Chapters 4 through 8 described the alternative model. It is driven by a definition of what it means to be educated. It has the teaching of six virtues as its purpose. It governs by modeling the six virtues, it structures itself as a community, and it takes an aesthetic approach to improvement.

This final chapter discusses four questions related to moving from our current model to the alternative:

- Why can't we keep our current model?
- How is the alternative model different from other reforms?

- What are the barriers to adopting the alternative model?
- How can the alternative model be adopted?

WHY CAN'T WE KEEP OUR CURRENT MODEL?

We must reject the current model for several reasons. The first is that our belief in democratic governance blinds us to the antieducational nature of current democratic practices, some of which were described in chapter 6. The health and survival of our democratic traditions depend on a system of public education that graduates virtuous, educated citizens, not vicious, uneducated ones.

Earlier chapters argued that, within our current model, we elect well-intentioned policymakers to direct public education toward shallow, uninspiring purposes. This happens because their interests are political and economic, not educational and philosophical. Public education can be governed educationally only when it is driven by a definition of what it means to be educated—a definition that emerges from philosophical discussion, not political debate.

The second reason to reject our current model is that children learn by watching adults. Public school governors and educators model and teach three virtues, but they also model and teach three vices. Public education cannot improve until those responsible for improving it demonstrate imagination, courage, and humility, in addition to understanding, strong character, and generosity.

The third reason to reject our current model is that two of its elements prevent the fundamental changes needed to improve schools. Public education has remained stable in spite of calls for its reform because both democratic governance and bureaucratic organizational structures are stabilizing forces. Neither promotes change or reform; and therefore, neither promotes improvement.

The fourth reason to reject our current model is that the social science improvement paradigm devalues imagination. Policymakers and school personnel need to understand school improvement ideas—but understanding without imagination cannot and does not improve anything. The art of school improvement requires the very kinds of imaginative actions that are devalued in our current model.

Finally, we must reject this model to get beyond the political debates that distract us from defining what it means to be educated. Educational politics engages educators and citizens in a dizzying array of debates concerning curriculum, teaching methods, funding, teacher pay, grouping students, and so forth. These debates take us to the periphery of public education and ignore the essential question of what it means to be educated.

The debate over student "tracking" is an example. Educators have long debated how best to group students for learning. Tracking proponents argue that high-achieving students should not be held back by slower ones. They also reason that low-achieving students should not be required to keep up with faster ones.

Arguments against tracking are based on research that found tracking sends negative messages to low-tracked students while not significantly improving the test scores of high-tracked ones. Tracking proponents counter with research that found high-tracked students benefit from homogeneous grouping.

Regardless of the weight of research evidence, tracking advocates usually win the debate by appealing to the commonsense idea that instruction can be more focused in classrooms of homogeneously grouped students. The argument is that, all other things being equal, efficiently focused instruction achieves higher test scores (a proxy for understanding).

The second reason tracking advocates win is that their position promotes strong character and generosity—the other two virtues taught in today's public schools. Teachers argue that students develop strong character in the competitive environments created by tracking. And those who teach in high-track classrooms model generosity by pushing students to achieve as much as they can. Those who teach in low-tracked ones model generosity in their willingness to work with struggling, unmotivated students.

This debate distracts us from doing what would be obvious, if we started with a deep, meaningful definition of what it means to be educated. If public education also valued imagination, courage, and humility, the debate would go away and so would tracking. The virtue combinations of *understanding and imagination, strong character and courage, generosity and humility* are developed best in heterogeneous classrooms. Here is why.

Students can explore questions about their education more imaginatively in heterogeneous classrooms than in homogeneous ones. Such classrooms are richer environments for asking and discussing the importance of what students are learning, to what extent it is important to different students, or why some students learn some things more easily than others. When educators value the development of imagination, students will be grouped heterogeneously, so these kinds of questions can be explored across a wide range of experiences and abilities.

The same is true when educators value the modeling and teaching of courage. Teachers asking the above questions model courage, and heterogeneous classrooms provide the best environment for students to explore them courageously with each other.

Humility is also more likely to be developed in heterogeneous classrooms. Proud teachers and students "think" they can teach and learn better in tracked classrooms. Humble ones are not threatened by "knowing" they can learn from those with different experiences and abilities.

The point is not to argue for either homogeneous or heterogeneous grouping. It is to illustrate that defining the educated person as one who develops all six virtues dissolves arguments about tracking, as well as other peripheral debates. Policymakers and school personnel simply need to model and teach the virtues. If students fail to achieve the desired results, the answer is always the same. Find new ways to build the virtue capacities of understanding, strong character, and humility; and find new ways to engage students in work that requires imagination, courage, and generosity.

As long as our current model is in place, public education will graduate citizens whose understanding is unimaginative, whose character is fearful, and whose generosity emerges from pride. Public education cannot be improved when the teaching of virtue is compromised in this way, no matter how many articles and books explain how to do it.

HOW IS THE ALTERNATIVE MODEL DIFFERENT FROM OTHER REFORMS?

Dissatisfaction with public education has prompted numerous calls for reform. Some call for specific purposes to be achieved through a detailed curriculum. Examples are magnet schools with arts-based or technology-based curricula. Some call for new approaches to governance. Examples are the charter school movement and voucher programs. Others build special organizational structures. For example, Comer Schools create teams of school personnel, parents, and community members. Still others design a curriculum around specific learning principles. Examples are Waldorf schools, based on the principle of developmental appropriateness.

Many of these reforms are achieving their purposes, but their successes and failures are not the subject here. The purpose of this section is to describe how the unique aspects of the alternative model make it different from all other reforms.

The first difference is that the alternative model addresses the essence of education. The introduction explained the importance of focusing on what is essential, and the six-virtue definition of the educated person gives this focus.

The introduction also mentioned that the five-element model of public schooling is another of this book's unique contributions. The second way the alternative model is different from all other reforms is that it takes into consideration the interrelatedness of all five elements.

We believe in the desirability of democratic governances, so we elect policymakers to establish educational purposes and to hire bureaucrats to hold teachers and principals accountable for accomplishing them. Teachers are expected to teach the content that is dictated at the local and state levels, and they are supposed to use the "best practices" found in educational research. Students move from grade to grade on the basis of satisfactory report cards and test scores, both of which are proxies for understanding the formal curriculum.

Exceptions to this description of school life prove the rule. Teachers can engage students in learning experiences other than those measured on standardized tests, but if standardized test scores are lower than desired, teachers are required to immediately focus on improving them.

Other reforms do not begin with a model that describes the relationships among the elements. Instead, they suggest new ways to govern, new purposes, new organizational structures, or new areas for research. None describe how the elements are interrelated.

The second difference is that the alternative recognizes how the American reverence for democratic governance drives everything. We never ask whether public schools should be governed democratically. It is simply assumed to be the best way to govern. To suggest otherwise is blasphemy.

The third way the alternative model differs from others is that it recognizes the antieducational nature of democratic governance. Many other reform-minded educators revere democracy, so they want to democratically govern in a way that is more educational than the ways described by Williams (2005). That is admirable, but our democracy has not evolved to where it models and promotes the virtues of the educated person.

It never will because the purpose of democracy is not to build an educated citizenry. That is the purpose of education. It cannot do so, however, as long as democratically elected officials model the vices of our uneducated nature. Everything about public education changes when a political core belief is replaced with an educational one.

The fourth way the alternative is different from other reforms is that it provides a virtue-based definition of the educated person. Others define the educated person as one who is academically knowledgeable and vocationally skillful. The knowledge and skills needed by society are constantly changing, so policymakers and school personnel speculate about what is needed in the future. The key word is "speculate" because we cannot know the future.

No such speculation is needed in the alternative model. It focuses on the question of what it means to be educated, so it prepares educated persons for all times. The six-virtue definition of the educated person focuses education on purposes that are simpler, more comprehensive, and more helpful than speculations about the specific knowledge and skills needed in the future. The six virtues have always been the mark of an educated person and they always will be.

In summary, the alternative model is unique because it starts with an explanation of how our current system works. It replaces a political core belief with an educational one, and it focuses public education on building a citizenry that is truly educated, not just knowledgeable and skillful.

WHAT ARE THE BARRIERS TO ADOPTING THE ALTERNATIVE MODEL?

My graduate students say, "The alternative model sounds great, but we can never operate that way. Everything about public education is political." I am full of hope when they say this because it means they see that the elements of our current model are integrally related to each other. I hope they also see that lasting improvement cannot occur until our current model is replaced by a model whose elements are similarly interrelated.

But I also get frustrated when they say this, and this frustration points to the main barrier to adopting the alternative model. My students reject the alternative model because they believe American public education must be governed politically. This belief prevents them from considering other governance approaches, even educational ones.

Beliefs are powerful drivers of thought and action, and two characteristics of beliefs make them difficult to change. The first characteristic is that holding onto our beliefs involves creating defenses against others.

Many years ago I was in the studio audience for a Wisconsin public television panel discussion. Before the panelists went on stage, moderator Dave Iverson came out to prepare the audience for what it would hear. Although abortion was not the panel discussion topic, he asked for a show of hands from those who believed in a woman's right to terminate a pregnancy. Then he asked for a show of hands from those who believed in a fetus's right to life. Finally he asked, "How many of you are willing to change your mind?" Not a single hand went up.

Believing something new often requires letting go of our existing beliefs—something we rarely do. But this needs to happen if the alternative model is to be adopted. My students' belief that we must govern politically does not make political governance necessary. It only means they hold a belief that prevents them from considering another way to govern. Only if they suspend their belief do other beliefs become possible. That was Iverson's point.

The second characteristic that makes beliefs difficult to change is that we profess them from our core. Examples are political beliefs. Our understanding of life is rooted in the beliefs that accompany and explain our experience. That is why the Fox News perspective rings true to Re-publicans and angers Democrats, and the MSNBC perspective does the same in reverse. Why do these shows cause such strong reactions?

We can try to see the world through a political perspective that con-tradicts our beliefs and experiences, but the effort quickly becomes tiresome. Republicans can't watch MSNBC without getting angry at what they consider distortions of their beliefs. The same is true for Democrats watching Fox News.

In other words, we feel a deep sense of ownership for our beliefs because, in the face of multiple possible beliefs, we choose them for ourselves. We own them in a way that may be more profound than any-thing else we own.

So the belief that public education must be governed politically is the main barrier to adopting the alternative model. And this belief is shared by elected officials, public educators, and citizens alike. Is this because they are democratically minded? Or is it because all three groups have interests that are served by our current model?

A public education system that promotes three virtues and three vices serves elected officials. Politicians do not conspire to keep voters intel-lectually incompetent, fearful, and proud; they simply benefit from a public school system that accomplishes it for them.

This is important because many Americans believe democratically elected officials are their leaders. When it comes to leading efforts to adopt the alternative model, however, citizens should realize that many elected officials have self-interested reasons to oppose it.

One reason is that this model fundamentally alters public educa-tion. It shifts from a focus on knowledge and skills to a focus on virtue. Elected officials rarely lead efforts that fundamentally alter the situation into which they were elected. Recent federal examples are ethics and campaign finance reforms. Both were passed after they were amended in ways that preserved the way Congress operates. Voting for these bills enabled incumbents to appear to be reformers as they voted for keeping things unchanged.

Another reason elected officials are likely to oppose the alternative model is that they, themselves, are governed by those who fund their reelection campaigns. Their first priority is to enable campaign con-tributors to remain powerful and prosperous. These powerful interests are safe with a citizenry that is intellectually incompetent, fearful, and proud.

A final reason elected officials are likely to oppose the alternative model is that a reverence for democratic politics blinds them to its anti-educational nature. Many consider it blasphemous to question the desirability of democratic governance, which is exactly the question posed in the alternative model.

In the end, it might be a good thing that politicians are likely to resist the alternative model. They often model human vices, so their behavior would only get in the way of achieving the alternative model's purpose, which is to model and promote a more virtuous citizenry.

A second group likely to oppose the alternative model includes those educators who believe public education's purposes should be strictly academic and vocational. Many teachers were good students themselves, so they value the kind of understanding for which they received good grades and earned high test scores. Their sense of being educated is reinforced by a focus on the same kind of academic and vocational understanding they demonstrated as students.

Teacher professional organizations are also likely to oppose the alternative model. Like other political interest groups, they are self-interested, so they resist reforms that increase responsibilities without higher pay. The alternative model increases teachers' responsibilities from modeling and teaching three virtues to modeling and teaching six. Therefore, teachers who would feel burdened by having to model and teach imagination, courage, and humility, in addition to understanding, strong character, and generosity are likely to pressure their unions to resist the alternative model.

A third group of resistors is likely to be those who participate in our consumer society. Advertisements and other promotional messages are everywhere because we are a nation of consumers. The accumulation of material possessions is highly valued in our society.

In the wake of the September 11 terrorist attack, President Bush asked Americans to go shopping. He had good reason to encourage this because our economy depends on the buying of things we want but don't need. As "accumulators" seek happiness in the acquisition of material possessions, they are oblivious to the need for a more educated citizenry.

Why is it important to recognize that the alternative model is likely to meet with strong opposition? Alternative model adopters need to realize that few school board members, state legislators, teachers, or fellow citizens recognize the need to replace our current model with the alternative. They also need to understand that opposition will come from many directions because the alternative model represents a fundamental shift in American education.

The strength of opposition is offset by the importance of replacing our current model with the alternative. The American experience during the latter part of the 20th century makes us the only affluent society in a position to promote virtuous living. Our recent economic experiences have taught us the dangers of "unchecked capitalism" (Gibboney, 2008), making us one of the few societies that can educate others about its dangers.

The Allied victory in World War II gave us significant economic advantages during the 1950s, 1960s, and 1970s. Our economy and standard of living became the dream of underdeveloped societies. That dream is now being realized by citizens of China, India, the former Soviet Union, and the Middle East. We must warn these emerging economic classes of the environmental and economic damage that can result from unchecked capitalism.

Our recent history has taught us that capitalistic excess threatens both our prosperity and the environment. If emerging economies fail to learn from our excesses, pollution and global warming are likely to change our planet in ways that will make 21st century global economic competition the least of anybody's concerns.

Before we can teach others about our experience, though, we must demonstrate that we have changed direction ourselves. The alternative model provides the best hope for changing direction. It does not reject capitalism, just its excesses. In fact, the health of both old and new capitalistic societies depends on the teaching and modeling of the six virtues.

The challenge for public education is to graduate citizens virtuous enough to build and maintain capitalistic economies that will not destroy the planet. There has never been a more important role for public education and a more important reason to change directions.

Another reason to anticipate opposition to the alternative model is to see who is left to adopt it. Just as some groups are likely resisters, others are likely adopters.

Parents dissatisfied with public schools are one such group. Many are looking for alternatives that offer fundamental, comprehensive schooling reform. The alternative model may appeal to them.

A second group is the teachers who have kept their idealism alive. Many teachers believe their role is to teach more than understanding, strong character, and generosity. Their idealism lies dormant, ready to emerge in schools that adopt the alternative model's definition of the educated person.

A third group is home-schooling parents. Many educate their young children at home, before sending them to public and parochial secondary schools as teenagers. They are likely to want their children's secondary schools to model and teach all six virtues.

Environmentalists and others concerned about unchecked capitalism are also likely to support reversing the direction of public education. Although capitalism has improved lives in many ways, many realize that it has denigrated human life in others. Environmental examples are smog, polluted rivers, and the increasing incidence of cancers. Psychic and social examples are alienation and the loosening of family bonds.

To summarize, alternative model proponents should recognize barriers to its adoption. The first is the difficulty of changing beliefs. Like political beliefs, educational ones are difficult to change. But in the end, they are just beliefs. Open-minded citizens can test their beliefs against experience and choose new ones, when experience dictates (Gardner, 2004). The second barrier is that our current model serves the interests of elected officials, teachers, their unions, and those who promote the consumerism that drives our economy. Members of these groups are likely to oppose the alternative model from many directions. Therefore, virtue-minded adults need to work together to adopt the alternative model for their children. The following section explains how this can be done.

HOW CAN WE ADOPT THE ALTERNATIVE MODEL?

One of my graduate students recently asked, "If you don't believe in the social science paradigm, why are you writing a book?" I was pleased with his insight. I was also alarmed that he might be right. If writing a book contradicts my argument against the social science improvement paradigm, my own argument is undermined in the very book in which it is made. Talk about irony!

Since that question was asked, another possible contradiction has occurred to me. If it is true that, "In all situations, it depends on the situation," why am I describing how to adopt the alternative model in this final section of chapter 9?

Here are my responses to both concerns. First, I address my student's question.

Yes—I reject the social science paradigm for improving schools. It is a dead end because it promotes *understanding* and ignores the other five virtues needed to improve schools. Its focus on understanding research findings, but obscures the need to bring *imagination, strong character, courage, humility,* and *generosity* to school improvement efforts.

But the question remains, "How is this book different from other school improvement books?" In the sense that all such books foster only one virtue (understanding), there is no difference.

That was my student's point. If I argue that understanding alone does not improve schools, why am I writing a book? He was astute in pointing out the contradiction, and he was right. This book will not enable readers to improve a school, even if this section describes hundreds of ways to do so.

But there is another way to answer my student's question. The main difference between this book and other school improvement works is that this is a philosophical treatise, not a social scientific one. This is the final chapter of a book in which I argue that research-informed political debates do not improve education because we have not yet defined what it means to be educated.

Howley and Howley (2007) also pointed out the need to have a clear sense of purpose:

> Perhaps the confusion of issues involving means and ends happens in education more often than we usually acknowledge. In the absence of worthy and widely endorsed aims, methods that might otherwise be adequate to the task can fail miserably. And if we tell ourselves that such failures result only from the use of ineffective methods, we might find that we're engaged in a never-ending but fruitless search for a "magic bullet"—the

sort of search that has arguably characterized the history of school reform in the United States for the last 100 or so years. (p. 347)

Endless debates about educational methods yield nothing because our educational purposes are not clear.

Therefore, to answer my student's question, I am writing this book to start a philosophical discussion about what it means to be educated. This purpose is consistent with my argument that we should stick to essential questions. Readers can decide the value of this book for themselves as they confront the question of what it means to be educated and as they work to improve education. Both are important, but the first must guide the second.

The other possible contradiction is in this final section of the last chapter. Describing how parents and teachers can adopt the alternative model seems to contradict the premise that, "In all situations, it depends on the situation."

To avoid this contradiction, I do not describe concrete ways to adopt the alternative model because that would undermine reader imagination and distract from the strong character, courage, humility, and generosity that are needed to improve any school situation. Instead, I pose three questions to guide those who are considering adopting the alternative model.

To pose these questions, I switch to second person and address them directly to you—the reader. Throughout this book, only my voice has been heard. The epilogue explains how other voices will be included in future discussions. The following letter to readers starts the discussion.

Dear Reader:

The following three questions can guide the adoption of the alternative model:

- Do you believe in the six-virtue definition of the educated person?
- Where can you find like-minded believers?
- Do your elected officials believe in this definition?

The first question asks if you can adopt a new belief, given the difficulty of suspending existing ones. The second follows from the discussion of those who are likely to be resisters and adopters. The third asks about the role of elected officials. Although policymakers may resist the alternative model, if citizens insist, democratically elected officials will listen and respond to citizen desires.

Do You Believe in the Six-Virtue Definition of the Educated Person?

Although the six-virtue definition appears simple, it raises complex, philosophical questions. Do you believe you are born ignorant, intellectually incompetent, weak, fearful, proud, and selfish? Do you believe you become educated as you develop understanding, imagination, strong character, courage, humility, and generosity? Do you believe understanding and imagination are the fundamental intellectual virtues; strength and courage are the fundamental character virtues; and humility and generosity are the fundamental spiritual virtues? Do you believe the six virtues make life beautiful and the six vices make it ugly?

Educational beliefs are based on both your reading about education and your experiences with learning and teaching. You cannot read about this definition anywhere else, so these beliefs must be tested in your experience.

You can do this by testing two premises against your experience. The first is that citizens with many years of schooling within our current model are unlikely to improve situations that require imagination, courage, or humility. The second mirrors the first. It is that you will be able to improve situations by modeling and promoting imagination, courage, and humility, as well as the understanding, strength, and generosity you learned in schools.

You can test the first by thinking about situations that can only be improved through the application of imagination, courage, and humility. For example, pretend you are a regional sales manager, and one of your sellers is not performing up to standard. Here is the context:

You graduated from a college in which you received a good training in the social sciences and humanities. Throughout your sales and management career, you have been an astute observer of human behavior, which enables you to understand others. This may be the reason you have been promoted twice.

Your early education was in public schools where you learned to value and demonstrate understanding, strong character, and generosity. You also learned to value those virtues in others. Your public school education also left you unimaginative, fearful, and proud; so you learned to value those vices in others, too. Middle managers often want subordinates to demonstrate both these sets of three virtues and three vices.

You recently hired both a woman and a man to join your sales force. Six months later, the woman's performance is almost up to that of the veteran salespeople, but the man's is not.

You are a direct person who wants to know why the salesman's performance is still low, so you call him to your office and ask why he is lagging behind his female colleague. As you listen and observe, your understanding is deepened by hearing the man's words and seeing his posture and mannerisms.

His answer and behavior suggest that he is intimidated. He seems fearful of losing his job, but you do nothing to lessen his fear because you believe fear is a good motivator, and motivating your new salesman is the reason for the conference. His fear also stimulates the pride you feel in being the boss.

Eventually, though, the man's fear makes you uncomfortable, so you offer to support him in any way you can. You are demonstrating the generosity you learned in school.

Finally, you tell him you had to work hard during your first year in sales, and he should do the same. You are encouraging him to bring strong character to the situation.

You don't explore the matter further because you are not imaginative, courageous, or humble enough to ask questions in a way that doesn't betray your authority over him. You want him to regard you as his boss, not his counselor.

This situation is wrought with fear, pride, and intellectual incompetence, some of which you bring to the situation and some of which the salesman brings. If these are the vices that created unsatisfactory performance, what is the likelihood that the performance will be improved without replacing these three vices with their opposite virtues?

Let's assume the salesman took your advice. He put in more time and effort, but he also remained unimaginative and fearful. What is the likelihood of improved sales?

On the other hand, what is the likelihood of improved sales, if imagination, courage, and humility replaced the vices that contributed to the low performance in the first place? Improvement is likely in the second case, but unlikely in the first.

But don't take my word for it. Test this first premise in your own experience.

To test the second premise, an education situation is presented. Here is the situation:

You are one of two teachers hired to replace two recently retired middle school physical education teachers. If you are male, you are the boys' PE instructor, completing your second year at the school. If you are female, you are the new girls' PE instructor, completing your first year. Both you and your colleague attended the same state university, which has a strong program in preparing physical education teachers.

Before the two of you were hired, your school's health and physical education program was limited to playing volleyball in the fall, basketball in the winter, and softball in the spring. Students have come to expect this routine. Many are not physically fit or athletic, so they lack enthusiasm for your health or physical education classes.

You and your colleague are discouraged by student attitudes, but you don't blame them. They are the victims. They get unhealthy messages from many of the adults around them, and even your fellow teachers send the message that health and physical education classes are the least important ones in school.

For the past year you shared your frustrations with each other. You realize programs like yours put health and physical education on the lowest rung of the curriculum. You and your colleague have decided to change that because nothing less than the lives of your students are at stake.

What should you do to make this situation better for the students in your school? If you believe in the six-virtue definition of the educated person, you believe the situation can be improved by modeling the six virtues and teaching students to be understanding, imaginative, strong, courageous, humble, and generous. You might try ideas and activities like the following:

First, to increase understanding, you set aside the first two days of summer vacation to discuss the current situation. You and your colleague share your observations and discuss what you learned in college about high-quality health and physical education programs.

From these discussions, you see the irony of working in a school district that has both a low regard for health and physical education and a large number of middle schoolers with diet, exercise, and diabetes problems. You conclude that, if you are going to improve the program, you need to change student and adult attitudes. You also remind each other not to blame the students. They are the victims—not the perpetrators—of this situation.

These understandings spark imaginative ways to address the situation. The following ideas emerge from your discussions:

- Many students are curious about their bodies, and some are interested in fashion. What about a unit that teaches about body types and how clothes influence their "look?"
- Action-animated computer games are popular with boys. What about a unit on their health effects? What about asking boys to create games that can be played in real space from those they play in virtual space?
- What do science classes teach about the human body? Is collaboration possible?
- Physical fitness is a big business. What links can be made with local gyms?

The possibilities are endless. You just have to be imaginative enough to find ways to implement them within the restrictive environment of a public middle school.

Strong character may be difficult to cultivate with this age group. Preadolescents are sensitive and insecure about their changing bodies. They are likely to reject any units or activities that might embarrass them. How can this be addressed? Maybe a unit can explore how other societies deal with this issue. Maybe this could be coordinated with a social science lesson.

In the end, modeling strong character may be the best way to teach it. You could point to older adolescents in the community who have demonstrated this virtue or ask students to nominate peers as examples of young people who have displayed strength of character.

Courage is also difficult to teach to this age group. Can students be challenged to engage in acts that are courageous but not dangerous? Such a unit might teach that different kinds of courageous action confront different kinds of fears. For example, a unit on square dancing might provide an opportunity for both boys and girls to overcome a fear of the other sex. Once again, the modeling of older adolescents might help teach this virtue.

The fifth virtue is humility. Many opportunities for building humility present themselves, if some of the previously posed possibilities become part of the program. Students need to draw from their reservoir of humility whenever they are challenged to do what they have never tried before. These experiences may teach them to appreciate the beauty of a humble spirit.

Finally, your new health and physical education program can teach generosity by expanding on the ways this virtue is already modeled by teachers. For example, implementing these ideas requires you to be generous with your time and effort. This will be obvious to students, and your generosity puts you in a position to expect and receive their generous efforts, in return.

Do you think taking these actions would improve the situation? It all depends on the situation, which means that funding, time, and other limitations come into play.

The more you look at situations this way, the more you can test the second premise. Depending on what you discover in these tests, your belief in the six-virtue definition of the educated person will be either reinforced or rejected.

You might object to this reasoning by saying, "Nobody questions that virtue makes things better. By definition, understanding, imagination, strength, courage, humility, and generosity make the world better. The problem is that people will always be both virtuous and vicious, and no amount of education will change that."

My response is that we will never know until we model and teach the ideals represented in the six virtues. Phenix (1961) makes the same point:

> If the schools, colleges, and universities are to serve as the mind and conscience of society, if they are to be sources of criticism, creativity, and guidance, it is imperative that they not be embedded in the regular administrative structure of government. Politics is the realm of collective ac-

tion; it is the art of the practicable; and the practicable is never the ideal. Education is the realm of individual exploration and creation; it is the transformation of practicality in the light of ideal possibilities. (p. 213)

If virtuous humans are an ideal, public education's purpose should be to teach that ideal. No other institution has this purpose, but public education does.

Where Can You Find Like-minded Believers?

If your belief in the six-virtue definition of the educated person is affirmed, your next step is to work with others who share this belief. The epilogue describes how to find those who share your belief. Internet technology makes this a simple matter.

Which Policymakers Share this Belief?

Your last step is to join with like-minded persons to elect policymakers who share your definition of the educated person. Political governance is likely to be with us for some time. Although politicians often demonstrate and promote vice, some might become proponents of the alternative model. At the local and state levels, it is still possible to elect politicians who realize that the purpose of education is to promote the development of all six virtues.

Our current model already teaches three virtues. It should not be difficult to convince policymakers and educators that imagination, courage, and humility are just as important as understanding, strong character, and generosity.

In summary, your first step is to challenge the six-virtue definition of the educated person. Test your experience to see if those who model and promote all six virtues make situations better. Then, find and work with others who share this belief. Finally, elect policymakers who believe in this definition too.

Sincerely,
J. Casey Hurley

The epilogue describes these last two steps in more detail.

EPILOGUE

Chapter 9 asks readers to test whether their experience affirms or denies the six-virtue definition of the educated person. This is easy to do with five of the virtues. It is easy to see that behaviors that emerge from understanding, imagination, strong character, courage, and generosity are likely to produce better outcomes than those that emerge from ignorance, intellectual incompetence, weak character, fear, and selfishness.

Modern definitions of humility and pride, however, make it difficult to think of humility as a virtue and pride as a vice. The first purpose of the epilogue is to explain why our modern definitions of humility and pride need to be reconsidered.

The second purpose is to explain the effects of neglecting imagination and courage in our schools. The third is to explain how readers can participate in discussions about how to improve education by modeling and promoting the six virtues.

This critique of American public education is partially based on three premises: Public education teaches the virtues of understanding, strong character, and generosity; public education also teaches the vices of intellectual incompetence, fear, and pride; and improving public education will require policymakers and school personnel to model and teach the virtues of humility, imagination, and courage. The next two sections

discuss this last premise, starting with the need to teach humility instead
of pride.

PUBLIC SCHOOLS SHOULD TEACH HUMILITY
INSTEAD OF PRIDE

Several months ago, I was drafting chapter 3, when my oldest son came
up to me and asked what I was writing, I told him I was defining the
six virtues of our educated human nature, and I told him my definition
each of virtue. Before continuing on his way, he said, "You have a lot
of explaining to do about that humility and pride thing. I don't think
people are going to get it."

As I talk to others, I realize he was right. I have a lot of explaining to
do to convince others that humility is a virtue and pride is a vice.

Medieval philosophers taught that pride is the first of the seven deadly
sins. Why do modern Americans consider it a virtue? Some might say
this is just semantics. Word meanings change through the ages. Once
considered a vice, pride is now a virtue. Meanings evolve. So what?

This is more than semantics and the evolution of meanings. If
pride were not so universally condemned at one time, and if it were
not so universally applauded now, we could say the meanings have
evolved. But meanings that have changed 180 degrees require a critical
examination.

Let's look at everyday uses of the word "pride." A sense of pride is
considered virtuous everywhere I look. For example, the banner hang-
ing at the entrance of my university says, "Proud to Be a Catamount."

And we expect bosses to be proud of their organizations and presidential candidates to be proud of their country. Barack Obama learned
the importance of expressing unwavering pride in his country after his
wife said she was proud of America for the first time in her adult life.
Candidate Obama knew that even a hint of inadequate pride would
devastate his run for the presidency.

In fact, during the campaign many argued that a lack of pride should
do just that. Americans expect the president to express unwavering
pride in the country, the military, and everything else associated with
America. It does not matter that some things about our country and its

actions throughout history are shameful. Candidates for public office must express pride in country, which is why candidate Obama took every opportunity to say he was a proud American.

I cringed every time I heard it. Did his multicultural experiences not teach him that the accident of birthplace is not something to be proud of? If pride is warranted by virtuous accomplishment, how is birthplace something to be proud of?

Candidate Obama expressed his pride in being an American because he was relating to the everyday meaning of pride—the pride we want to see in our leaders, the pride we feel in being Americans, and the pride expressed on our university banners. These are not related to accomplishments, but they are about relationships with others. We want to be associated with others who have accomplished great things. Our pride is fed by this desire.

Another everyday meaning of pride is expressed when a superior says to a subordinate, "I am proud of you." When a teacher says this to a student, a mother to a child, or a boss to an employee, the first effect is that the superior shines a light on a subordinate's accomplishment. The second effect is the reinforcement of the superior–subordinate relationship. In other words, statements of pride in subordinates also shine a light on superiors. How is it virtuous to shine a light on your superior relationship with a subordinate?

This second effect is illustrated by contrasting the message that is sent when a superior expresses pride in a subordinate with the message that is sent when a subordinate says to a superior, "I am proud of you." In the second case, a single light shines on the accomplishment of the superior because the expression of pride is unrelated to the relationship.

This is a matter of deep meaning, not just semantics. Those who express pride in the accident of birthplace or in a university affiliation shine a light on themselves, as much as on the birthplace or university. And an expression of a superior's pride in a subordinate's accomplishment shines a light on the relationship as much as on the accomplishment of the subordinate.

We don't see that these everyday expressions of pride are not virtuous because we don't understand how humility is a virtue. When a superior's recognition of a subordinate's accomplishment is changed to "I am humbled by your accomplishment," the virtuousness of humility is apparent. This language shines a single light on the accomplishment, not the relationship. It suggests that all human beings can make the world better, and it suggests that such accomplishments deserve recognition. The accomplishment is unrelated to the relationships involved in the recognition. In fact, the virtue of humility expresses itself in the ability to shine a light on the accomplishments of others.

So why does public education teach pride instead of humility? The main reason is that humility is completely misunderstood. True humility is based on a sense of goodness so profound that the humble person does not need the recognition of others. Those who only "think" they are good, but don't "know" it to their core, need a reassuring light on themselves. Those who are secure in their goodness use it in the service of others as they shine a light on others' accomplishments.

Humble people bring beauty and appreciation into the lives of many people, but proud ones cannot. Everywhere I look, humility is needed to improve education, but pride is planted firmly in the way. Pride in birthplace or university affiliation blinds one to the merits of other birthplaces or affiliations. And an expression of pride in a subordinate's accomplishment casts a shadow from the light that shines on the superior's position.

Medieval philosophers were right. They described pride as a vice because of what it said about man's relationship with God. It is still a vice today, because it is a powerful barrier to improving the lives of those without power.

NEGLECTING IMAGINATION AND COURAGE

Imagination and courage are the other neglected virtues. Public schools not only fail to teach them, but they also devalue them as they emphasize understanding and fear.

Public education's obsession with standardized test scores illustrates the value placed on understanding. This obsession cannot be disputed. Almost every study of effective schools assumes that "effectiveness" is related to achieving high standardized test scores. This obsession teaches students that correct answers, which are a proxy for understanding, are so important that promotion to the next grade depends on them. Students are also taught that their future depends on them.

Teachers value the right answer so much that they neglect imagination, which renders students intellectually incompetent. The result is that our graduates are unable to take imaginative action to use what they understand.

The result of this intellectual incompetence is that imagination is devalued in the larger society too. Over the past 25 years, I have attended countless meetings with all sorts of educators on all sorts of topics. We consistently promote fuller, deeper, more comprehensive understandings of problem situations, but we rarely search for more imaginative ways to approach them. I have rarely been in meetings in which the purpose was to come up with imaginative new ways of thinking or doing something, but I have often attended meetings in which the purpose was to convey and promote a common understanding. Educators seem to regard understanding as essential, but imagination as dangerous.

Likewise, public school personnel consistently model and teach fear. As mentioned in chapter 7, schools exist on the edge of chaos, so it is natural for teachers to fear losing control to a student body that outnumbers them 20 to 1.

At the start of their careers, teachers learn two things at the same time. First, they learn that maintaining an orderly classroom is a challenge that is both professional and personal. They struggle to be knowledgeable enough, imaginative enough, strong enough, courageous enough, humble enough, and generous enough to connect with students who are sometimes reluctant and uncooperative.

As beginning teachers engage in this struggle, they also learn that nothing is more important than having an orderly classroom. This learning is constantly reinforced by parents, colleagues, and superiors. In this way, losing control of the classroom becomes every teacher's greatest fear. And this fear is modeled to students, whether teachers recognize it or not.

As teachers grow and develop, they overcome this fear, but it invariably resurfaces whenever student rebellion threatens their control of the classroom or school. For example, school administrators model and teach this fear as they work to prevent student unrest from becoming public protest. The reason for the unrest is less important than the need to prevent protest, resulting in the modeling of fear to both teachers and students.

Fear is also taught through the elaborate system of rules that is supposed to control student behavior. Public educators have established an educational system that mimics our civil system of laws, courts, and prisons. One of public education's purposes is to teach students to fear the consequences of violating school rules, so they become adults who fear violating society's rules.

The teaching of fear, however, also carries with it the lost opportunity to teach courage. If public schools had a virtue-based set of purposes, they would teach that bold actions are virtuous when they emerge from understanding, strong character, and generosity, but they are cowardly when they emerge from ignorance, weakness, and selfishness. Instead, public school personnel have chosen to maintain safe, orderly environments by teaching students to fear the consequences of rule violations.

Teachers and administrators realize school environments are fragile, but they don't realize that their fragility is caused by teaching fear instead of courage. Public schools would not be so fragile if teachers modeled the courage that emerges from strong character, understanding, and generosity; and if they taught students to develop the same kind of courage.

In summary, one step toward improving public schools is to understand the need to teach humility, imagination, and courage. They are neglected virtues, not because they are difficult to teach but because our definition of the educated person does not regard them as equal to understanding, strong character, and generosity. This can be remedied by promoting the philosophical discussions that should be part of any system of education.

GIVE YOUR VOICE TO THE ALTERNATIVE MODEL MOVEMENT

This book concludes by requesting reader participation in just such philosophical discussions. In order to participate in discussions about the alternative model, go to the following URL: http://www.sixvirtues.com

If you believe in the six-virtue definition of the educated citizen, submit the "Join Six Virtues" form that identifies you as a believer. This will take less than one minute.

You can also check the "Roster" to see who else shares your belief. The "Roster" is a state-by-state listing of other believers. We expect the list to grow, so check it often.

This book does not offer specific ways to move from our current model to the alternative because it is a philosophical treatise. I have studied K–12 schools for the past 20 years, but I no longer work in them. Therefore, I want readers to share their stories about how aspects of the alternative model and the six virtues are at work in their careers and lives. The stories shared by readers of this book will provide the "how to do it" part of adopting the alternative model that will be told in the next book.

To present a story for consideration in the next book, simply click on "Share a Story." Provide your name and phone number, and I will call to schedule a time to record it for telling in the next book. Before anything goes to print, you will have final approval on your story's presentation.

REFERENCES

Allington, R. (2005, February). Ideology is still trumping evidence. *Phi Delta Kappan*, 86(6), 462–468.

Anyon, J. (2005). *Radical Possibilities: Public Policy, Urban Education, and a New Social Movement*. New York: Routledge.

Armstrong, T. (2006). *The Best Schools*. Alexandria, VA: Association for Supervision and Curriculum Development.

Bates, R. (1984). Toward a critical practice of educational administration. In T. Sergiovanni & J. Corbally (Eds.), *Leadership and Organizational Culture: New Perspectives on Administrative Theory and Practice* (pp. 260–274). Urbana: University of Illinois Press.

Bell, T. (1993, April). Reflections one decade after *a Nation at Risk*. *Phi Delta Kappan*, 74(8), 592–597.

Bellamy, G. T., & Goodlad, J. I. (2008, April). Continuity and change: In the pursuit of a democratic public mission for our schools. *Phi Delta Kappan*, 89(8), 565–571.

Berliner, D. (2005). Our impoverished view of educational reform. *Teachers College Record*, 108(6), 949–995. Retrieved November 24, 2008, from http://www.tcrecord.org (ID Number: 12106).

Biddle, B., & Berliner, D. (2002, May). Unequal school funding in the United States. *Educational Leadership*, 59(8), 48–59.

Boyd, W. L. (1989). The political economy of public schools. In Joel Burdin, (Ed.) *School Leadership: A Contemporary Reader* (pp. 204–224).

Bracey, G. (2003, April). April foolishness: The 20th anniversary of *A Nation at Risk*. *Phi Delta Kappan*, 84(8), pp. 616–621.

Bracey, G. (2008, October). The 18th Bracey Report on the condition of public education: Schools-are-awful bloc still busy in 2008. *Phi Delta Kappan*, 90(2), 103–114.

Brandt, R. (1992, February). On rethinking leadership: A conversation with Tom Sergiovanni. *Educational Leadership*, 46–49.

Brown, J. L., & Moffett, C. (1999). *The Hero's Journey: How Educators Can Transform Schools and Improve Learning*. Alexandria, VA: Association for Supervision and Curriculum Development.

Brubaker, D., & Nelson, R. (1974). *Creative Survival in Educational Bureaucracies*. Berkeley, CA: McCutchan.

Brulle, A. (2005, February). What can you say when research and policy collide? *Phi Delta Kappan*, 96(6), 433–437.

Bryk, A., Lee, V., & Holland, P. (1993). *Catholic Schools and the Common Good*. Cambridge, MA: Harvard University Press.

Cavanagh, S. (2008, June 24). Since NCLB law, test scores on rise [Electronic version]. *Education Week*, 27(43).

Calhoun, C. (Ed.). (2002). *Dictionary of the Social Sciences*. Oxford: Oxford University Press. Retrieved June 16, 2005, from *Oxford Reference Online* at http://www.oxfordreference.com/views/ENTRY.html?subview=Mainandentry=t104.e1220

Clinton, B. (2005). *My Life: The Early Years*. New York: Vintage Books.

Cochran-Smith, M. (2002, September–October). The research base for teacher education: Metaphors we live (and die) by. *Journal of Teacher Education*, 53(4), 283–285.

Comte-Sponville, A. (2001). *A Small Treatise on the Great Virtues*. Trans. Catherine Temerson. New York: Metropolitan Books.

Cuban, L. (1984). *How Teachers Taught: Constancy and Change in American Classrooms, 1890–1980*. New York: Longman.

Cuban, L. (2003). *Why Is It So Hard to Get Good Schools?* New York: Teachers College Press.

Davis, S. H. (2007, April). Bridging the gap between research and practice: What's good, what's bad, and how can one be sure? *Phi Delta Kappan*, 88(8), 568–578.

De Pree, M. (1989). *Leadership Is an Art*. New York: Doubleday.

Dewey, J. (1938). *Experience and Education*. New York: Macmillan.

Dufour, R., & Eaker, R. (1998). *Professional Learning Communities at Work: Best Practices for Enhancing Student Achievement*. Bloomington, IN: National Education Service.

Dufour, R., Eaker, R., & Dufour, R. (2005). Recurring themes of professional learning communities and the assumptions they challenge. In R. Dufour, R. Eaker, & R. Dufour (Eds.), *On Common Ground: The Power of Professional Learning Communities* (pp. 7–29). Bloomington, IN: Solution Tree Press.

Dyer, W. (1976). *Your Erroneous Zones*. New York: Funk & Wagnalls.

Elkind, D., & Sweet, F. (2007a). In search of character. Retrieved May 14, 2009, from http://www.livewiremedia.com/allguides/ISOC-1.pdf http://www.livewiremedia.com/isoc.html

Elkind, D., & Sweet, F. (2007b). How to do character education. Retrieved August 13, 2007, from http://www.goodcharacter.com/Article_4.html (Originally published as "You Are a Character Educator," *Today's Schools,* September–October 2004)

Elmore, R., & Fuhrman, S. (1994a). Governing curriculum: Changing patterns in policy, politics, and practice. In R. Elmore & S. Fuhrman (Eds.), *The Governance of Curriculum: 1994 Yearbook of the Association for Supervision and Curriculum Development* (pp. 1–10). Alexandria, VA: Association for Supervision and Curriculum Development.

Elmore, R., & Fuhrman, S. (1994b). Education professionals and curriculum governance. In R. Elmore & S. Fuhrman (Eds.), *The Governance of Curriculum: 1994 Yearbook of the Association for Supervision and Curriculum Development* (pp. 210–215). Alexandria, VA: Association for Supervision and Curriculum Development.

Emmons, R. (2007). *Thanks: How the Science of Gratitude Can Make You Happier.* Boston: Houghton Mifflin.

Fullan, M. (2005). Professional learning communities writ large. In R. Dufour, R. Eaker, & R. Dufour (Eds.), *On Common Ground: The Power of Professional Learning Communities* (pp. 209–223). Bloomington, IN: Solution Tree Press.

Garan, E. (2002). *Resisting Reading Mandates: How to Triumph with the Truth.* Portsmouth, NH: Heinemann.

Gardner, H. (2000). *The Disciplined Mind.* New York. Penguin Putnam.

Gardner, H. (2004). *Changing Minds: The Art and Science of Changing Our Own and Other People's Minds.* Boston: Harvard Business School Press.

Germeraad, S. (2008, January 17). Too many states consistently spend less money in school districts educating English language learners, low-income students and students of color. *Education Trust Press Release.*

Gibboney, R. (2008, September). Why an undemocratic capitalism has brought public education to its knees: A manifesto. *Phi Delta Kappan,* 90(1), 21–31.

Golden, K. C. (2004). The inevitability trap. In Paul Rogat Loeb (Ed.), *The Impossible Will Take a Little While: A Person's Guide to Hope in a Time of Fear* (pp. 344–345). New York: Basic Books.

Goodson, I., & Foote, M. (2001, January 15). Testing times: A school case study. *Education Policy Analysis Archives,* 9(2). Retrieved September 10, 2007, from http://epaa.asu.edu/epaa/v9n2.html

Graham, P. (2005). *Schooling America: How the Public Schools Meet the Nation's Changing Needs.* New York: Oxford University Press.

Greenfield, T. B. (1986). The decline and fall of science in educational administration. *Interchange,* 17(2), 57–80.

Hargreaves, A. (2008). Leading professional learning communities: Moral choices amid murky realities. In A. Blankstein, P. Houston, & R. Cole (Eds.), *Sustaining Professional Learning Communities* (pp. 175–197). Thousand Oaks, CA: Corwin Press.

Highet, G. (1989). *The Art of Teaching*. New York: Vintage Books (Originally published 1950).

Hord, S., & Hirsh, S. (2008). Making the promise a reality. In A. Blankstein, P. Houston, & R. Cole (Eds.), *Sustaining Professional Learning Communities* (pp. 23–40). Thousand Oaks, CA: Corwin Press.

Howley, A., & Howley, C. (2007). *Thinking About Schools: New Theories and Innovative Practice*. Mahwah, NJ: Lawrence Erlbaum.

Hurley, C. (2002, December). Art and human potential. *Principal Leadership*, 24–27.

Hurley, C. (2005, February 20). Inequality of school funding should shame N.C. legislators. *Asheville Citizen-Times*, A11.

Kneller, G. F. (1994). *Educationists and Their Vanities: One Hundred Missives to My Colleagues*. San Francisco: Caddo Gap Press.

Kohn, A. (2006, September). Abusing research: The study of homework and other examples. *Phi Delta Kappan*, 88(1), 8–22.

Loviglio, J. (2007, January 27). Brain researchers study science behind spirituality. *Asheville Citizen-Times*, E3.

Lyon, L., Lubin, I., Meriam, L., & Wright, P. (1931/1968). Whither the social sciences. In *Essays on Research in the Social Sciences: Papers Presented in a General Session Conducted by the Committee on Training of the Brookings Institution, 1930–31* (pp. 3–8). Port Washington, NY: Kennikat Press.

MacIntyre, A. (1981). *After Virtue: A Study in Moral Theory*. Notre Dame, IN: University of Notre Dame Press.

MacIntyre, A. (1999). *Dependent Rational Animals: Why Human Beings Need the Virtues*. Chicago: Carus.

Manzo, K. (2007). E-mails reveal federal reach over reading: Communications show pattern of meddling in "Reading First." *Education Week*, 26(24), 1, 18.

Marzano, R. (2003). *What Works in Schools: Translating Research into Action*. Alexandria, VA: Association for Supervision and Curriculum Development.

Marzano, R. (2007). *The Art and Science of Teaching: A Comprehensive Framework for Effective Instruction*. Alexandria, VA: Association for Supervision and Curriculum Development.

Mathews, J., & Helderman, R. (2004, February 9). Educators decry law's intrusion, not its cost: "No Child" rules rile Va. officials. *Washington Post*, B-1.

McClintock, R. (2007, March 28). Educational research. *Teachers College Record*. Retrieved March 21, 2008, from http://www.tcrecord.org (ID Number: 13956)

Moore, T. (2000). Religion. In M. Williamson (Ed.), *Imagine What America Could Be in the 21st Century: Visions of a Better Future from Leading American Thinkers* (pp. 299–313). Emmanus, PA: Daybreak/St. Martin's Press.

Morris, T. (1997). *If Aristotle Ran General Motors: The New Soul of Business.* New York: Henry Holt.

Morris-Young, D. (2007, July 27). Clarifying the church's teachings. *Catholic News and Herald*, 16(35), 1, 7.

Morrison, C. (2003, December 24). Grad stats incomplete, N.C. says. *Asheville Citizen-Times*, C1.

National Council of Churches Committee on Public Education and Literacy. (2007). Ten moral concerns in the implementation of the *No Child Left Behind Act*. Retrieved April 30, 2007, from http://www.ncccusa.org/pdfs/LeftBehind.html

Palmer, P. (1994). Leading from within: Out of the shadow into the light. In J. Conger (Ed.), *Spirit at Work* (pp. 19–40). San Francisco: Jossey-Bass.

Parker, W. (2005, January). Teaching against idiocy. *Phi Delta Kappan*, 344–351.

Peck, M. S. (1978). *The Road Less Traveled: A New Psychology of Love, Traditional Values, and Spiritual Growth.* New York: Simon & Schuster.

Peck, M. S. (1987). *The Different Drum: Community Making and Peace.* New York: Simon & Schuster.

Phenix, P. (1961). *Education and the Common Good: A Moral Philosophy of the Curriculum.* New York: Harper & Row.

Pinchot, G., & Pinchot, E. (1993). *The End of Bureaucracy and the Rise of the Intelligent Organization.* San Francisco: Berrett-Koehler.

Pink, D. (2006). *A Whole New Mind: Why the Right-Brainers Will Rule the Future.* New York: Riverhead Books.

Rhee, M. (2007). Interviewed by Brian Lamb; Q and A—CSPAN, aired September 9, 2007. Uncorrected transcript provided by Morningside Partners. Retrieved September 11, 2007, from http://q-and-a.org/Program/?ProgramID=1144

Rothstein, R., Jacobsen, R., & Wilder, T. (2006, November 29). "Proficiency for all" is an oxymoron. *Education Week*, 26(13), 32, 44.

Sahakian, W. (1968). *History of Philosophy.* New York: Barnes & Noble Books.

Sarason, S. (1990). *The Predictable Failure of Educational Reform: Can We Change Course Before It's Too Late?* San Francisco: Jossey-Bass.

Scherer, M. (2007, May). Why focus on the whole child? *Educational Leadership*, 64(8), 7.

Schmoker, M. (1996). *Results: The Key to Continuous School Improvement.* Alexandria, VA: Association for Supervision and Curriculum Development.

Schmoker, M. (2004, February). The tipping point: From feckless reform to substantive instructional improvement. *Phi Delta Kappan*, 424–432.

Schmoker, M. (2005). No turning back: The ironclad case for professional learning communities. In R. Dufour, R. Eaker, & R. Dufour (Eds.), *On Common Ground: The Power of Professional Learning Communities* (pp. 135–153). Bloomington, IN: Solution Tree Press.

Schmoker, M. (2006). *Results Now: How We Can Achieve Unprecedented Improvements in Teaching and Learning.* Alexandria, VA: Association for Supervision and Curriculum Development.

Schmoker, M. (2007, April). Reading, writing and thinking for all. *Educational Leadership*, 63-66.

Sternberg, R. (1996). *Successful Intelligence: How Practical and Creative Intelligence Determine Success in Life.* New York: Simon & Schuster.

Stoll, L., Bolam, R., McMahon, A., Wallace, M., & Thomas, S. (2006). Professional learning communities: A review of the literature. *Journal of Educational Change*, 7, 221–258.

Tyack, D., & Hansot, E. (1982). *Managers of Virtue.* New York: Basic Books.

Wallis, C. (2008, February 25). How to make great teachers. *Time*, pp. 28–34.

Wheatley, M. (2007). *Finding Our Way: Leadership for an Uncertain Time.* San Francisco: Berrett-Koehler.

Williams, J. (2005). *Cheating Our Kids: How Politics and Greed Ruin Education.* New York: Palgrave Macmillan.

Winfield, N. (2007, July 11). Pope: Other churches defective. *Asheville Citizen-Times*, A1.

ABOUT THE AUTHOR

J. Casey Hurley is a professor of educational administration at Western Carolina University. He served as secretary of the Faculty Senate from 1996 to 2000, and chair of the faculty from 2000 to 2002. He also coordinates the university's master of arts in education degree program in Jamaica and other international sites.

He earned a bachelor of arts in English from St. Norbert College, DePere, Wisconsin, and a master's degree in educational administration from the University of Wisconsin–Madison, after which he served as an assistant principal and principal in three Wisconsin public high schools. He earned a PhD from UW–Madison in 1989.

He started teaching and coaching early in life. While a high school junior and senior at Xavier High School in Appleton, Wisconsin, he was the instructional assistant for the city's summer youth baseball program; and he coached sixth- and seventh-grade basketball at St. Joseph Grade School. He returned to Xavier High to teach English and coach basketball and baseball from 1974 to 1977, before starting a career in educational administration.